ANNOUNCING THE
NOW IN PREPARATIO:

The edition of *The Complete Works of Frances Ridley Havergal* has five parts:

Volume I   *Behold Your King:*
           The Complete Poetical Works of Frances Ridley Havergal

Volume II *Whose I Am and Whom I Serve:*
           Prose Works of Frances Ridley Havergal

Volume III *Loving Messages for the Little Ones:*
           Works for Children by Frances Ridley Havergal

Volume IV *Love for Love: Frances Ridley Havergal:*
           Memorials, Letters and Biographical Works

Volume V   *Songs of Truth and Love:*
           Music by Frances Ridley Havergal and William Henry Havergal

David L. Chalkley, Editor   Dr. Glen T. Wegge, Music Editor

The Music of Frances Ridley Havergal by Glen T. Wegge, Ph.D.

This Companion Volume to the Havergal edition is a valuable presentation of F.R.H.'s extant scores. Except for a very few of her hymn scores published in hymn-books, most or nearly all of F.R.H.'s scores have been very little—if any at all—seen, or even known of, for nearly a century. What a valuable body of music has been un-known for so long and is now made available to many. Dr. Wegge completed his Ph.D. in Music Theory at Indiana University at Bloomington, and his diligence and thoroughness in this volume are obvious. First an analysis of F.R.H.'s compositions is given, an essay that both addresses the most advanced musicians and also reach-es those who are untrained in music; then all the extant scores that have been found are newly typeset, with complete texts for each score and extensive indices at the end of the book. This volume presents F.R.H.'s music in newly typeset scores diligently prepared by Dr. Wegge, and Volume V of the Havergal edition presents the scores in facsimile, the original 19th century scores. (The essay—a dissertation—analysing her scores is given the same both in this Companion Volume and in Volume V of the Havergal edition.)

    Dr. Wegge is also preparing all of these scores for publication in performance fo-lio editions.

A portrait of F.R.H., taken by the photographers Elliott and Fry in London, on Saturday, February 1, 1879, seven weeks after her 42nd birthday.

Love for Love.

1 JOHN 4:16.

KNOWING that the God on high,
   With a tender Father's grace,
Waits to hear your faintest cry,
   Waits to show a Father's face,—
Stay and think!—oh, should not you
Love this gracious Father too?

Knowing Christ was crucified,
   Knowing that He loves you now
Just as much as when He died
   With the thorns upon His brow,—
Stay and think!—oh, should not you
Love this blessèd Saviour too?

Knowing that a Spirit strives
   With your weary, wandering heart,
Who can change the restless lives,
   Pure and perfect peace impart,—
Stay and think!—oh, should not you
Love this loving Spirit too?

Frances Ridley Havergal

This next hymn was found in *God Is Love; or, Memorials of Little Nony*, a small book published in Volume IV of this Havergal edition. The author is not known, likely not F. R. H.

I.

Lord, look upon a little child,
By nature sinful, rude, and wild;
Oh! put Thy gracious hands on me,
And make me all I ought to be.

II.

Make me Thy child, a child of God,
Washed in my Saviour's precious blood;
And my whole heart from sin set free,
A little vessel full of Thee.

III.

A star of early dawn, and bright,
Shining within Thy sacred light;
A beam of light to all around,
A little spot of hallowed ground.

IV.

Dear Jesus, take me to Thy breast,
And bless me that I may be blest;
Both when I wake and when I sleep,
Thy little lamb in safety keep.

A Song in the Night.

[Written in severe pain, Sunday afternoon, October 8th, 1876, at the Pension Wengen, Alps.]

I take this pain, Lord Jesus,
    From Thine own hand,
The strength to bear it bravely
    Thou wilt command.

I am too weak for effort,
    So let me rest,
In hush of sweet submission,
    On Thine own breast.

I take this pain, Lord Jesus,
    As proof indeed
That Thou art watching closely
    My truest need:

That Thou, my Good Physician,
    Art watching still;
That all Thine own good pleasure
    Thou wilt fulfil.

I take this pain, Lord Jesus,
    What Thou dost choose
The soul that really loves Thee
    Will not refuse.

It is not for the first time
    I trust to-day;
For Thee my heart has never
    A trustless 'Nay!'

I take this pain, Lord Jesus,
    But what beside?

'T is no unmingled portion
    Thou dost provide.

In every hour of faintness,
    My cup runs o'er
With faithfulness and mercy,
    And love's Sweet store.

I take this pain, Lord Jesus,
    As Thine own gift,
And true though tremulous praises
    I now uplift.

I am too weak to sing them,
    But Thou dost hear
The whisper from the pillow,—
    Thou art so near!

'T is Thy dear hand, O Saviour,
    That presseth sore,
The hand that bears the nail-prints
    For evermore.

And now beneath its shadow,
    Hidden by Thee,
The pressure only tells me
    Thou lovest me!

Frances Ridley Havergal

BRUEY:

A LITTLE WORKER FOR CHRIST.

"WHOSE I AM, AND WHOM I SERVE."

AND

THE

FOUR HAPPY DAYS.

BY

FRANCES RIDLEY HAVERGAL.

"Knowing her intense desire that Christ should be magnified, whether
by her life or in her death, may it be to His glory
that in these pages she, being dead,
'Yet speaketh ! ' "

Taken from the Edition of *The Complete Works of Frances Ridley Havergal.*

David L. Chalkley, Editor   Dr. Glen T. Wegge, Associate Editor

ISBN 978-1-937236-12-0   Library of Congress: 2011940452

Book cover by Sherry Goodwin and David Carter.

CONTENTS.

LIST OF ILLUSTRATIONS.

"Come over and Help Us."

The Irish child's cry.

OH, children of England, beyond the blue sea,
Your poor little brothers and sisters are we;
'Tis not much affection or pity we find,
But we hear you are loving and gentle and kind;
So will you not listen a minute or two,
While we tell you a tale that is all of it true?

We live in a cabin, dark, smoky, and poor;
At night we lie down on the hard dirty floor;
Our clothes are oft tattered, and shoes we have none;
Our food we must beg, as we always have done;
So cold and so hungry, and wretched are we,
It would make you quite sad if you only could see.

There's no one to teach us poor children to read;
There's no one to help us, and no one to lead;
There's no one at all that will tell us the way
To be happy or safe, or teach us to pray:
To the bright place above us we all want to go,
But we cannot,—for how to get there we don't know.

They tell us the Virgin will hear if we call,
But sure in one minute she can't hear us all.
And the saints are too busy in Heaven, we hear;
Then often the priests make us tremble with fear
At the fire of purgatory, which, as they tell,
Is almost as dreadful as going to hell.

Oh, will you not help us, and send us a ray
Of the light of the Gospel, to brighten our way?
Oh, will you not tell us the beautiful story
Of Jesus, who came from His dwelling of glory
To save little children, and not only you,
But even the poor ragged Irish ones too?

The English Child's Reply.

WE have heard the call from your fair green Isle;
  Our hearts have wept at your saddening tale;
And we long to waken a brighter smile
  By a story of love which shall never fail.

We should like you to come to our Bible-land,
  And share our comforts and blessings too;
We would take you all with a sister's hand,
  And try to teach and to gladden you.

But you're so far off that it cannot be,
  And we have no wings, or to you we'd fly;
So we'll try to send o'er the foaming sea
  Sweet words to brighten each heavy eye,—

Sweet words of Him, who was once so poor,
  That He had not where to lay His head;
But hath opened now the gleaming door
  To the palace of light, where His feast is spread.

There you may enter; He calls each one,—
  You're as welcome there as the greatest king!
Come to Him then, for He casts out none,
  And nothing at all do you need to bring.

He will change your rags for a robe of white,
  An angel-harp, and a crown of gold;
You may dwell for aye in His presence bright,
  And the beaming smiles of His love behold.

We will gladly save from our little store
  Our pennies, our farthings, from day to day,
And only wish we could do far more;
  But for Erin's children we'll always pray.

A Plea for the Little Ones.

It was Easter Monday morning,
  A dull and showery day;
We were sorry for the children
  Who could not run and play.

I heard the sound of singing
  As I passed along the street—
An unseen tiny chorus
  Of tiny voices sweet.

Beneath a sheltering doorway,
  Safe from the April weather
Eight happy little singers
  Sat lovingly together,

Five crowding on the doorstep
  With arms entwined, and three
On broken stool or baby chair,
  Close clustering knee to knee.

They sang about the " happy land,"
  So very " far away,"
And happier faces never shone
  In any game of play.

And then they sang it all again,
  And gently rocked each other;
Then said the little leader,
  " Now let us sing another!"

" Now *I* will say a hymn to you!"
  (Oh, the sixteen eyes were bright!)
So I said them " Little Jessie,"
  As they listened with delight.

JESSIE'S FRIEND.

" Little Jessie, darling pet,
  Do you want a Friend?

One who never will forget,
    Loving to the end?
One whom you can tell, when sad,
    Everything that grieves,
One who loves to make you glad,
    One who never leaves?

"Such a loving Friend is ours,
    Near us all the day,
Helping us in lesson-hours,
    Smiling on our play;
Keeping us from doing wrong,
    Guarding everywhere;
Listening to each happy song,
    And each little prayer.

"Jessie, if you only knew
    What He is to me,
Surely you would love Him too,
    You would "come and see."
Come, and you will find it true,
    Happy you will be!
Jesus says, and says to you,
    'Come, oh come, to Me.'"

———————

"Now tell me who, if you can guess,
    Was little Jessie's Friend?
Who is the Friend that loves so much,
    And loveth to the end?"

I would that you had seen the smile
    On every sunny face;
It made a palace of delight
    Out of that dismal place,

As, reverently yet joyously,
    They answered without fear,
"It's Jesus!" That belovèd Name
    Had never seemed more dear.

And then we talked awhile of Him—
 They knew the story well;
His holy life, His precious death,
 Those rosy lips could tell.

All beautiful, and wonderful,
 And sweet and true it seemed,
Such hold no fairy tale had gained
 That ever fancy dreamed.

So, to be good and kind all day
 These little children tried,
Because they knew *He* was so good,
 Because *He* bled and died.

Blest knowledge! Oh, what human lore
 Can be compared with such!
"Who taught you this, dear little ones?
 Where did you learn so much?"

Again the bright eyes cheerily
 Looked up from step and stool;
They answered (mark the answer well!),
 "*We learnt it all at school!*"

At school, at school! And shall we take
 The Book of books away!
Withhold it from the little ones?
 Leave them at will to stray—

Upon dark mountains, helplessly,
 Without the guiding light
That God entrusts to *us,* until
 They perish in the night?

What was the world before that Book
 Went forth in glorious night?
Availed the lore of Greece and Rome
 To chase its Stygian night?

We send the messengers of life
   To many a distant strand.
And shall we tie the tongues that teach
   The poor of our own land?

Shall husks and chaff be freely given,
   And not the Bread of Life?
And shall the Word of Peace become
   A centre of mad strife?

Shall those who name the Name of Christ
   His own great gift withhold?
Our Lamp, our Chart, our Sword, our Song,
   Our Pearl, our most fine Gold!

Why would ye have "no Bible taught"?
   Is it for *fear?* or shame?
Out, out upon such coward hearts,
   False to their Master's name!

If God be God, if truth be truth,
   If Christian men be men,
Let them arise and fight the fight,
   Though it were one to ten!

With battle-cry of valiant faith,
   Let Britain's sons arise,—
"Our children *shall* be taught the Word
   That only maketh wise!"

So, dauntlessly, will we unfurl
   Our banner bright and broad,
The cause of His dear Word of Life,
   Our cause, the Cause of God.

BRUEY:

A LITTLE WORKER FOR CHRIST.

"WHOSE I AM, AND WHOM I SERVE."

BY

FRANCES RIDLEY HAVERGAL,

AUTHOR OF "LITTLE PILLOWS" AND "MORNING BELLS."

New Edition.

LONDON:

JAMES NISBET & CO., 21 BERNERS STREET.

MDCCCLXXX.

The title page of Bruey *published by Nisbet in 1880.*

LITTLE BRUEY.
The illustration at the front of the 1880 Nisbet edition.

BRUEY:

A LITTLE WORKER FOR CHRIST.

"WHOSE I AM, AND WHOM I SERVE."

BY

FRANCES RIDLEY HAVERGAL,

AUTHOR OF "LITTLE PILLOWS" AND "MORNING BELLS."

New Edition.

LONDON:
JAMES NISBET & CO., 21 BERNERS STREET.
MDCCCLXXX.

TO

ALICE AND BERTHA,

WITH

AUNT FANNY'S LOVE.

CONTENTS.

"We know five texts now, one for every finger."

James Nisbet & Co. was F.R.H.'s primary publisher, and their edition of Bruey *is the one with the frontispiece on page 8 of this book. Another edition of* Bruey *was published by the American Sunday-School Union of Philadelphia, having this illustration at the front of the book. See page 30 of this book.*

BRUEY:

A LITTLE WORKER FOR CHRIST.

CHAPTER I.

HOW BRUEY BEGAN HER WORK.

Four and twenty minutes past nine by the clock of St. Mary's Sunday school, Rilverton, on a sunny Sunday morning in early spring.

A little girl came in with a lady teacher. She had dark hair and rosy cheeks, and looked remarkably strong and well. You would have noticed her ready and pleasant smile, and her pretty way of looking up brightly when any one spoke to her. At other times there was a thoughtful look on her face, not at all sad, but as if she had a great deal to think about, and very important business on hand. She would have told you that she would be " twelve next birthday."

"Here's little Miss Murray," whispered Emma Fayling, a girl in the second class. "Look! mother goes charing to Mrs. Murray's, and she likes Miss Bru-ey."

"What a funny name!" said Alice Fosbery, who sat next. "But do see what a pretty hat she has. That's just what *I* should like—that wreath all round."

"Perhaps she is coming to sit with our class: see Miss Anstey is come in with her, and now they are gone up to speak to Miss Allison. I hope she'll come."

Alice kept her eyes on the hat. "Yes, I hope she will; but I'm afraid she is going to teach some of the little ones. I wonder if that wreath is very dear. I *do* like it. I wonder if I could get a rose like that for a shilling—the biggest, I mean—that one in front."

"Why, what good would it be if you did? You wouldn't be let wear it; and you wouldn't like to be sent home to take it out if you'd got it in a new hat on Whitmonday."

"No, I know it's no use thinking about it; but I should like it, all the same. At Lizzie Telf's school, they let them wear what they like; and Lizzie got her mother to let her have such lovely pink flowers, only last Saturday week, and she did up her old hat with them till it looks fit for any lady. I met Rosa coming to school, that lives in her street, and she says she's crying this morning because she can't go to school and wear it."

"Why not?" asked Clara Jones.

"Oh, because her shoes are got so bad, and let the water in; and Rosa says there's a hole in one that a stone got in and made her foot quite sore."

"Well," said Clara, "I know what I'd soonest have had, if I'd been Lizzie."

Just then Miss Anstey came to her class, the girls rose and curtsied, and the talking was at an end; but Emma and Alice kept looking at Bruey, till Clara reminded them that there were only two minutes more before the bell would ring, and that they had not looked over their collects.

Whilst this had been going on, Bruey's friend, Miss Anstey, had led her up to Miss Allison, the Superintendent.

"If you have many of those very little ones to-day, my little friend Bruey would be delighted to try and teach a few of them, if you will trust her."

The Superintendent said, "I daresay Miss Denton will be very glad to give her three or four of her little girls, for so many new ones have come in lately that her class is getting too large, and yet there are hardly enough to divide it into two classes." Then a few kind words were spoken to Bruey, about how nice it would be if she would try to tell the little ones something about Jesus, and all the kind and wonderful things He did; and how much the Superintendent hoped that Bruey herself loved Jesus, and would try to teach them for His sake. Bruey did not speak a word. She only looked very grave, and listened, with her great dark eyes fixed on the kind face. And she followed very quietly, and slowly, when Miss Allison said, "Come with me, dear, and I will find you something to do among the tiny ones."

Very soon Bruey was seated on a stool, with a little bench before her, on which were four little girls of six or seven years old. She had a text to teach them, and a Bible story to tell them. Whenever the Superintendent looked that way, she saw the four little heads looking straight before them at the little teacher, and there was much less noise from that corner of the room than when Miss Denton had her whole class to manage.

After school was over, Bruey was brave enough to walk right across the room to her, and say, "Please, may I come this afternoon?"

"Yes, dear, I shall be quite glad if you will. But they are always more troublesome in the afternoon; will it not tire you too much to come again?"

"No, I shall not be tired," said Bruey, "if I may come."

So it was settled; and then Bruey walked soberly back to her little girls, and made them sit perfectly still till the word was given to take places, two and two, for walking to church. "Eighth class!" and at the word Miss Denton and her little girls stood up and went to their places, and Bruey and her little girls followed them. All the way to church she walked beside them, leaving them at the door to go to her mother's seat.

In the afternoon she was at school before her children, but they soon came in, and went straight to her without any further orders. After school, the Superintendent came to her and said—

"Well, Bruey, are you tired?"

"No."

"Have your children been good?"

"Yes; very!"

"And did you try to teach them about Jesus?"

There was no answer to this. Bruey was not shy about most things, but she felt very shy about saying anything about herself. But she looked up and smiled, which was perhaps as good as an answer, and presently she said—

"May I come again next Sunday?"

She was not likely to get a "No" to this, so she went home with plenty to think about, both as to the Sunday that was nearly over, and as to the Sundays that were to come.

Bruey had no father; he had died when she was only six years old. She lived with her mother, in the middle of a long and pleasant row of houses, a little way out of the town, all enclosed by an iron gate, opening upon a broad gravel path, with houses on one side, and little sloping gardens on the other. Her only sister, Ada, was at a foreign school, and was not to come home till next Christmas, so Bruey would have been alone with her mother, but for a cousin who boarded with them, and went to the Rilverton grammar school. Cousin Percy, who was nearly two years older than Bruey, had come after the Christmas holidays, and had not yet, according to his own account, succeeded in "making out" this new plaything or puzzle, as he regarded his little cousin. But "girls always are queer even if they are ever so jolly," remarked Percy, and liked her all the better for not being too comprehensible. He came in to tea, just as Bruey had answered her mother's question by saying, "Oh yes, mamma, I walked with Miss Winter and Miss Anstey all the way to the turning just below the gate. Miss Winter says I may always come back with them; but I like walking by myself best."

"That's Bruey all over! Aunt, only imagine what Bruey must have suffered in permitting me to walk with her all the way to the primrose wood! Next time

I've that honour, I'll remember her taste. Bruey, how far off will do? Suppose I keep thirty yards ahead; will you graciously reckon that walking by yourself?"

"I did not mean always," returned Bruey, quite seriously.

"Well, how many of your young ladies can say the alphabet backwards? Any of them forward enough for that?"

"I don't teach them any letters; they learn that on week days."

"What! not A, B, C, D?" mocked Percy, in excellent infant school drawl. "Aunt, I hope you will take care Bruey doesn't get at any books on Sunday."

Bruey took no notice of this, but answered, "You don't learn your Greek verbs on Sunday; and that's just the same."

"Just the same as A, B, C! I wish it was. But come now, Bruey, tell us all about it. What do you do when they are obstreperous? Box their ears all round? Or one at a time? Tell you what, you had better charter me to come along with you, and keep order. They would be quiet for at least ten minutes, if I did this,"—"this" being illustrated by a most horrible and astonishing grimace, which had frightened Bruey herself the first time she saw it. But she was used to Percy now, and understood him a great deal better than he understood her. "Then you could hold forth, you know, till the effect passed off, and then, if they got restive, I could repeat the dose. Now, Bruey, listen to reason, and don't refuse good offers; would not this be a great advantage?"

"It's very kind of you, but I think I'll wait till I have seen you keep still ten minutes yourself, first; because I should not like my children to get bad marks by mistake for you."

Percy always enjoyed bringing out the comical curve of Bruey's mouth, which accompanied the little hits which he delighted in bringing upon himself.

"I'll be such a good boy, Bruey!"

"You don't mean to say so!" she replied, playfully. "Mamma, really those little things are so good. I do like them. I was so afraid Miss Allison would not want me next Sunday. But she will, and she says I may have the same children again;—I was so glad. Isn't it curious, one of them is poor Mrs. Fayling's little girl, Bella. And another lives next door to her—Hetty Fosbery, such a funny little thing. That is where you lend tracts, don't you, mamma? Might I go with you some day?"

"We will see. Did you find out where the others live?"

"No, mamma."

"Then you had better ask them next Sunday. I don't promise that you shall go and see them, that must depend upon circumstances; still, if you find out all you can about them, it may be a good thing for them, and for you too."

"For me too, mamma?"

Mrs. Murray smiled, but did not explain. "Perhaps you will find that out when you have taught them longer."

After tea, Bruey rose to leave the room. Percy was tumbling about on the sofa. "Don't be horrid, and go away just when a fellow's got nothing to do but to tease you. Come here, and tell us some more about these young ones."

"I don't want to stay now, Percy, if you don't mind."

As Bruey shut the door, Percy said, "Whatever made her take a fancy to go to the Sunday-school? I hope she'll soon be tired of it."

"I don't think she will, said Mrs. Murray, quietly.

"She is a funny one. Aunt, what a great girl she is for her age. She must be a head taller than my little sister Jessie. But she can't run a bit; never saw a worse hand at it; Jessie could beat her out of sight. She's strong in the wrist, though."

"Don't tease her to run, Percy; it is not good for her."

"I thought it always did girls good, the same as boys Why, what a muff a fellow would get if he always went slow train."

"It is not good for Bruey, because she had rheumatic fever when she was quite a little thing, just before your dear uncle died; and ever since that, though she has been strong and well in all other respects, she has never been able to run fast without losing her breath, and once or twice it has brought on palpitation. So never persuade her to run, that's a good boy."

Percy was quite alive to the altered tone which Mrs. Murray's voice took when she alluded to his uncle; but it is harder for boys than for girls to show any sort of sympathy with the sorrow of older persons, so it was not because he was unfeeling that he went on.

"Aunt, why do you call her 'Bruey'? It's such a queer name, one can't tell whether it is masculine or feminine."

"That was her dear father's doing. We called her 'Baby' till she was beginning to talk, and then he used to try to teach her to say 'Ellen Bruce Murray,' and she *would* say 'Bruey' for 'Bruce' so funnily and prettily, that he took to call her 'little Bruey,' and then the rest of us did. And I could not call her anything else now, because "—

She did not finish the sentence, but looked out and away at the sunset, and beyond it.

Percy was silent too.

Meanwhile, Bruey sat by the window of a little room above, and watched the sunset too. It was her mother's dressing-room, but had been gradually resigned to Bruey, till it was as good as her own. She slept in the adjoining room with her mother, but it was here that she always finished dressing and said her prayers; going out through the door opening upon the landing, that she might not disturb her mother, if ready first, as she often was. There was a little table by the window, and a chintz-covered box beside it. A folded rug upon this box made it soft and comfortable for a seat. This was the corner where she always said her prayers; she liked being able to look up at the sky then. On this box she sat, with her feet curled up under her, leaning her arms on the table, just tired enough to enjoy doing nothing.

It was a clear, lovely evening, very still, with that soft tone over everything which makes one feel it is spring before a bit of green is to be seen in any hedge. The view was pleasant, and Bruey was never tired of it; over the sloping garden, and between the trees at the bottom; over the town below, with church towers and one tall spire; and then a range of western hills, dark purple now, against the clear sky where the sun had just gone down. For a little while she only gave herself up to the quiet beauty of the sunset. Then she ran over the day, long looked forward to, nearly over now; she had really taught in the Sunday-school, and was really to go on with this new work.

It seemed rather serious. She recollected what Miss Allison had said about hoping that she herself loved the Lord Jesus. She hoped she did; but *did* she? A few months ago she was quite sure she did; she had loved Him very much then, and remembered having knelt at her little window in the autumn twilight on more than one Sunday evening, as she did now in the spring twilight, and feeling very happy, and wishing she could do anything in the world to please Him, and show Him that she loved Him. But *now?* It was not quite the same. She had read her Bible every morning and evening just the same, but she somehow never came now to any verses that seemed so very sweet and beautiful as then. And she had not missed saying her prayers, but there was not the same pleasure in it, and other things would keep coming into her head. She had not given up a custom, then begun, of coming upstairs alone, and reading and praying a little while, after tea on Sunday evenings, till the bells began to ring for evening service; but she had done it lately more because she felt uncomfortable if she did not, than because she really loved to be "alone with Jesus."

She felt softened, and sorry, and tender, this evening, and wished she could feel all the love she once did. She had tried to tell her little girls about it. Was that right, when she did not feel it herself? But she wanted them to feel it, and that could not be wrong. Still, it was almost like being a hypocrite, and that was so dreadful. She never meant to be that, and did not think she ever had been before. If she was to be a teacher, she ought to be better; but instead of that she was worse, for this was something quite new. And yet, suppose one of those little girls were to die, and she had never tried to tell them about Jesus!

What should she do? It was not the first time Bruey had done the only thing that could do any good. She had "told Jesus" all that troubled her more than once before. Especially once, when she told Him that she felt very sinful, and could not make herself any better, and wanted very much indeed to be saved and forgiven; and then words that His own lips said long ago seemed to come into her mind,—"Thy sins be forgiven thee,"—and she felt as if a great load were lifted from her heart.

So now she slid down from the box, and knelt beside it, and "told Him all that was in her heart." It was a long story, but she knew He would listen to it all; and as the sunset faded away, the light within grew brighter, and Bruey was, indeed, a happy little girl, seeking and finding peace in Jesus.

She was still kneeling when the bells began to ring out. She rose just as her mamma opened the door between the two rooms, and said, "Bruey, are you sure you are not too tired to go to church to-night?"

"Oh, dear no, mamma! I was a little bit tired after tea, but I am not tired now, and it is such a nice evening. I would much rather go, please."

CHAPTER II.

HOW BRUEY WENT ON WITH HER WORK.

THREE or four Sundays after this, Bruey sat on her little stool, with an empty little form before her, for it was early yet. She liked being early, for she came to know her little girls so much better by it. When school had once begun, there could be no talking. But when she was first, and Mary and Hetty and Sophy and Bella came in one by one, she could see that they came across the room quietly, and made a nice curtsy, and then she could have quite a nice talk with each; and the little girls liked this so much, that the "Eighth Class, Second Division," began to make a most creditable appearance in the attendance book, having no half-marks for coming late, instead of whole ones for coming in time.

But Miss Allison, the good Superintendent, was there even before Bruey. For she had long found out the same thing, and a few early words with one and another of the teachers had often made all the difference between good and bad, or earnest and lifeless, teaching. Miss Allison saw Bruey sitting alone, and went at once to speak to her. She had something to say which she wished she need not say, and yet she felt she ought to say it. Bruey rose and shook hands with her, and smiled as usual; and a very lovable smile it was. Miss Allison put her hand very lovingly on her shoulder, and said—

"Bruey, dear, I am sure you will not think I mean it unkindly if I ask you to do something which, perhaps, you will not quite like. Will you?"

"Oh no, Miss Allison!" And she looked up in great wonder as to what could possibly be coming. Could Miss Allison be going to ask her not to come to school any more? Oh, she hoped not! But Miss Allison's face did not look exactly like *that*.

Miss Allison hesitated. Though Bruey was only a little girl, she did not wish to vex her, and she wanted to tell her this thing, which she, perhaps, would not like, nor be able to understand the reason for, as gently and winningly as possible.

"What is it? You are not going to send me away?"

"Oh no, darling, never! But, dear little one, tell me, would you not be sorry if you did just a little harm when you might do only good?"

"Oh, yes! But what?" And Bruey, who seldom spoke many words, said so much with her eyes, that Miss Allison saw she had better tell her quickly, lest Bruey might fancy something much worse was coming.

"Well, darling, it is only this. Next time you have a new hat, will you ask your mamma to let you have a neat one, without gay flowers on it? It might be very nice and pretty, you know, without them."

Bruey looked very much astonished.

"I will try to tell you why, dear. It is one of the printed rules of the school that the children are not to wear flowers. But you see, Bruey, if they see the teachers wearing them, they will want to wear them too. So we try to set them a good example, and show them that we can dress very nicely without being smart and gay. When Miss Lester comes in, just notice how nice she looks, and yet how quiet and neat; and then notice her class, those great girls, they all look so nice and neat too. They have all agreed to have white ribbon on their bonnets this spring, instead of all sorts of gay colours."

Just as plainly as if she had spoken, Bruey's face said that she did not quite understand what difference it could make whether they wore flowers or not, though the simple white trimming was unquestionably prettier than old smart flowers.

So Miss Allison went on. "See, Bruey, dear, if they once begin to want to wear smart flowers, they tease their poor parents to buy them when they cannot afford it, or waste their own little earnings on them, instead of doing something better with their money. And then they think a great deal about it, and are tempted to be vain and foolish, and to care about what they wear much more than anything else, and to be envious of other girls who have managed to get finer things still. Will this help them or hinder them, do you think, as to seeking after better things?"

Bruey looked as if she had got something new to think about.

"So, dear Bruey, we want to save them from being tempted thus, and so the rule about neat dressing was made; and then, what do *you* think? don't you think it is best for us, too, not to wear what they are forbidden! If they see that we do not care about fine clothes, it will help them a little not to care either, and they are not so likely to want to break the rule."

Bruey looked as if she would like to say something, but had not quite courage.

"There is just one other thing I want to say; don't you think that if you do this it will please the Lord Jesus? Not that it matters to Him; but He will know all about it, and know that you would like to give up anything which might hinder any little girl from thinking about her soul and about her Saviour. It seems a very little thing, but you might do it for His sake; and I know He would be pleased—really *pleased*, Bruey!" She said the last words very softly, and bending her face down, with a loving look and tone, as if she were asking this little thing for the sake of a Master beloved indeed.

It was totally new to Bruey. And it was her way to be quite silent when she heard anything quite new.

But she had listened, and would remember almost every word.

"I have not vexed you, dear, have I, by asking you to do this?"

"Oh no, indeed! but I did not know. Thank you for telling me, dear Miss Allison."

Eight minutes yet before the clock hand would show half-past nine, and the bell ring, and the door close. Which three things always happened exactly together, as the children very well knew, and the teachers too. Little Hetty Fosbery trotted in.

"Good morning, Hetty."

"Good morning, teacher."

"You did not come so early last Sunday, Hetty, so you have never told me who else there is at home besides Alice. Have you another sister?"

"No, teacher, there's only Willie."

"And is Willie a big boy?"

"No, teacher; he isn't hardly as big as me, and he can't walk; but he's very old. He'll be twelve years old come next Christmas. Alice is going in fourteen, and I'm going in seven."

"How is it Willie can't walk; is he ill?" asked Bruey.

"Please, teacher, his legs is weak and all drawn up, so as he can't stand; and his back's all growed out."

"Poor Willie! are you not very sorry for him?"

Hetty had always seen Willie like that, and it was just a matter of course that he should not be able to run about; so she had never thought of being sorry for him, except once, when a rude boy upset the little chair in which he sat outside the door in warm weather; and Willie, not being able to save himself, fell on a sharp stone, and Hetty saw blood trickling down his white forehead.

"I should be so sorry for him if he were my brother. How he must want to run about and play, like you do! Does he ask you to fetch him what he wants, Hetty?"

"Yes, teacher." But this was said very low, and Hetty's eyes went down on her shoes. Yes, Willie did ask her sometimes to fetch him what he could not reach, and sometimes Hetty did, and sometimes Hetty didn't. So she thought Miss Bruey must know somehow, and she felt ashamed of herself, and hoped Willie would ask her to go all the way upstairs for something directly she got home, that she might do it, and get rid of an uncomfortable feeling that she ought to have been kind and sorry for Willie, like Miss Bruey.

"But I want to know some more about Willie. What does he do all day?"

"Please, teacher, he'll read all day long, if he can get any books; and if he can't, he frets. But he didn't fret much last week, for mother gave him twopence to be a good boy, and Alice got him some blue and red paint with it, and mother let him have the ink, and he drawed ever such a lot of pictures, and that kept him from pining after the books."

"Where does he get books from?"

"He hitches himself along in his chair to the neighbours, and they lets him have them if they've got any, else a piece of newspaper will do—he can read anything. But sometimes he's a good while together that he seems poorly like, and can't hitch his chair at all, and then he'll read his old ones what he's got in a box, till he's done them all again, and then he frets, till mother don't know what to do."

Hetty looked round, and caught sight of Bella and Sophy through the open door. "Teacher, I'll tell you a secret before they come. Alice said I mustn't tell Bella Fayling, 'cause she lives next door, and she'd tell. Alice is going to get Willie a box with ever such a lot of paints in, what he can make pictures with, and not fret; she's going to have a shilling for marking things at school; she got ninepence of it on Friday; and it's such a beautiful box, it will cost almost all that."

"That *will* be nice, and how pleased Alice will be to give it him. Good morning, Bella! good morning, Sophy! Did you say your text to Grannie last Sunday, Bella?"

"Yes, teacher."

"And did Grannie like it?"

"Yes, teacher."

"What did Grannie say about it?"

"I don't know, teacher."

"Please, teacher," struck in Hetty, who was always ready to answer for herself and for everybody else too, "Bella's Grannie said—'cause I was by, and helped Bella say it right"—

"Now, stop a minute, Hetty. I want Bella to tell me herself; you shall tell me something else. What was it, Bella?

"Said her learnt it when her was a little girl," said Bella, shyly.

"It was a good lady taught it her," said Hetty, "and she knows it now, and said it after me and Bella."

"How nice!" said Bruey. "I wonder if you will remember your texts when you are old women. You will try to learn a great many, won't you? And, Bella, I wonder whether Grannie will know the text we are going to learn to-day; perhaps she will, and then she will be pleased again. We will try and get it very perfect, so that you can say it right off to her."

"I'll help her," said Hetty, very patronisingly. "I can say all the texts—four. I said them twice over to Willie. And the hymn too."

Sophy Willis, a pale little thing, stood waiting her turn, with evidently something to communicate. "Please, teacher, mother says 'Thank you, and baby's cough's better.'"

"Oh, I'm so glad!" said Bruey. "I know that stuff Mamma gives me always does my cough good, and I hope it will quite cure your baby's. Is it all gone, Sophy?"

"No, teacher, there's some in the bottom of the bottle."

"When it is finished, Mamma says you may come up for some more, if it does baby any good."

"Please, teacher, mother didn't give it all to baby; our little Jim coughs too, and he had some of it to stop him coughing in the night, 'cause he woke baby and father."

"Come early in the morning, Sophy, when you come for more, because I might be gone out for a walk if you come later, and then I could not give it you myself."

Sophy's washed-out little eyes, that were often open half the night with the coughing babies, looked quite bright at this; she had sometimes gone to ladies' houses for things kindly promised to her mother, and had felt so frightened at the fine servants, who either did not speak to her at all, or only told her to "mind she didn't break the jug, else she'd catch it," that she would willingly have gone at four o'clock in the morning to ensure Miss Bruey coming to give her the bottle of cough mixture her own self.

Miss Allison's eye was on the clock, and before Sophy's eyes got dull again the hand touched the half-hour, and the bell was rung, and the door was shut. All who came after that moment had to wait outside till prayers were over, when the door was opened to admit any late-comers

"Teacher," said Hetty, after prayers, "there's Mary Shelton! And she's a-crying."

Little Mary came to her place with such a sorrowful drag in her little feet, that you did not need to look above her ankles to know that something was the matter. Little children's feet have a great deal of expression. There is often as much temper shown in the toes as in the tongue. Don't you know a sulky child's walk! And how pretty it is to see merry feet and legs! And comfortable, good-tempered ones!

I don't know whether Bruey noticed the feet, but she could not help seeing the tears, and the wet fingers that acted pocket handkerchief.

"What is the matter, dear? Is it because you are late? Never mind, I am sure you did not mean to be, and next Sunday will soon come, and then you will be sure to be in time, won't you?"

"I should have been in time, teacher, but—oh, dear!" And the fingers did duty again, as aforesaid.

"But what, dear?"

"I catched my frock on a nail, coming by that boarding, and tore him all along—see, teacher!" and Mary displayed a great compound tear in a poor, thin little dress, evidently made up to "do for Sundays," out of some old barège[1], not fit for children's wear. "And mother said her'd mended him so often, her shouldn't mend him no more, and if I tore him again I must stop at home." After which sorrowful tale it was very plain that it was only the knowledge that she "mustn't make a noise," which kept the sobs from breaking into a howl.

Bruey drew the poor little thing nearer to her, and looked very minutely and sympathisingly at the torn frock. "Have you no other frock, Mary, that you could come in?"

"Only my cotton one, and he's so dirty, and mother hasn't time to wash him. But I'd come in that, only mother wouldn't let me, I know. Mother will be so angry; her'll beat me."

"Don't cry. I don't think she will. You tell her teacher doesn't want her to be angry with you this time. Come, you won't be able to see the little picture I have brought if you don't stop crying."

But it would not do; Mary still sobbed, and the morning's work could not be begun till she was quieted. Bruey did not quite know what to do, so she just did nothing for a minute or so,—that is, nothing but think. The thinking was to some purpose, for she suddenly recollected that Miss Allison thought that the Lord Jesus knew and noticed even such little things as dress; and if He knew about hers, He must know about this poor little crying child's torn frock. Bruey had never ventured to speak to any one else about Jesus, and it was very difficult even with these little girls, though not so hard now as at first. But she tried.

[1] barège: a silky material

"Mary, hush a minute, dear; does anybody else know you have torn your frock?"

"No, teacher, only Emma Fayling; she pinned it up for me."

"Somebody else does know, though; Somebody very kind and good, that loves little Mary, and is very sorry when she is sorry. Shouldn't you like to know who, Mary?"

Mary stopped crying, because she could not think who else but Miss Bruey could possibly know, and Hetty leant forward, all smiles and curiosity. She was a child of quick imagination, and began wondering if it was some rich lady who would buy Mary a new frock.

"*Jesus* knows, Mary."

Hetty looked half disappointed. Mary gave a great clearing-up sniff and sob, and looked up at Bruey to hear more. Would it make any difference if He did know? Perhaps it would.

"Dear little Mary, the Lord Jesus saw you all the while, and saw you tear your frock, and watched you crying all the way to school, and I know He is sorry when any of His little children are sorry and cry. He knows how badly it is torn, and all about it. Didn't I tell you last Sunday how much He loves His little children?"

"Yes, teacher."

"And how kind and good He is to the little children that pray to Him?"

"Yes, teacher."

"Now, I think if we were to ask Him He would comfort you—I mean, make you feel less sorry, and help you to feel happy again; and I think we might ask Him about mother, too, mightn't we?"

"Yes, teacher," was said again, though Mary did not quite understand what could be asked "about mother."

Bruey looked at the others to make sure that they were quietly listening, and then she put her hands together, and said, "O Lord Jesus, Thou knowest how sorry Mary is that she has torn her frock; we ask Thee to comfort her, and not let her feel so sorry any more about it; and when she goes home, oh please keep her mother from being very angry, and do not let her beat Mary. Do hear us, Lord Jesus, and show us how good and kind Thou art. Amen."

Mary was quite quiet now, and Hetty was sobered down; neither of them had ever heard anybody speak to Jesus before just as if He were there to listen. Little Sophy looked up to the skylight in the roof, following Bruey's lifted eyes, as if she half expected to see something.

"There now, Mary, we have told the Lord Jesus all about it, and you will feel so much better, and you'll see mother won't beat you. But now, who can say last Sunday's text?"

"I can!" said Hetty.

"Me!" said Mary.

Sophy put out a rather uncertain finger, signifying that she was not sure. Bella had hers in her mouth.

"Does not Bella know it? oh I am sure she does. Now think, Bella, what you said to Grannie." Whereupon it seemed to dawn upon Bella, and she took her finger out of her mouth, and stretched her hand straight out, signifying, "I know it."

"Now, answer all together by hands out. Who knows the text?" And the four hands were stretched out.

Hetty began, "Come unto"—

"Stop, Hetty!" Bruey raised her hand. "Stand!" Of course Hetty was up in an instant, and Bella was last.

"That won't do. It was not all together. Try again. Now—*sit!*" As Bruey smiled, the little girls smiled too, and even Bella seemed to like it.

"Now, all together, *very* softly—*stand!*" It was "all together" this time, but not "very softly," for Sophy's boots made too much noise, and Hetty pushed the form a little.

"We must try again; I think they could hear us in the next class, and they must not hear us at all, you know. See who can be the quietest. Now—*sit! stand!*"

And this time it was "all together," and quite softly. Bruey looked pleased. "There, that was beautiful!" she said, at which the children were delighted.

"Now, once all together, very softly, 'Come——'"; and they repeated in a measured undertone the words which Bella's Grannie had learnt sixty years ago, "Come unto me, all ye that labour, and are heavy laden, and I will give you rest."

Then each said it alone, Bruey having some difficulty to keep Hetty from prompting the others; then twice all together again; then those who had not said it quite perfectly before, tried again, till at last all had it perfect.

"Now, the text of the Sunday before—'Wash——'"; and the little girls took it up, "Wash me, and I shall be whiter than snow."

"Now, the one before that, 'Christ——'"; "Christ Jesus came into the world to save sinners."

"Bella did not say it. Come, Bella, you can say that so nicely, try!" After one or two reminders, Bella did say it nicely, and then "all together" again.

"Now, the very first we learnt, 'We love——'"; "I like that one best," said Hetty very fast, managing to get the words out in time to chime in with "We—love—Him—because—He—first—loved—us."

"Now, I wonder if we couldn't say them all off without stopping?" and Bruey lowered her voice and led the little girls in softly repeating all their four texts. It seemed quite a feat to them.

"There, wasn't that nice! What a number you will know if you come every Sunday; for we won't forget any of them. I've such a pretty new one to teach you. You shall say it after me two or three times first, and then I'll tell you about it." They repeated after Bruey, "The foxes have holes, and the birds of the air have nests, but the Son of Man hath not where to lay His head."

"Sit!" It was quietly done this time, so Bruey began at once—

"You never saw a fox; but I saw one once. He was something like a dog, and he had reddish-brown fur, and very bright, black eyes, and a beautiful bushy tail."

"Teacher, I've seen one."

"You, Hetty?"

"Yes, teacher; Willie showed me one in a book, and there was some quite little ones too."

"Ask Willie to show it you again, and Bella too, and then you can say to him the text about the foxes. Well, the foxes are not tame like the dogs are, and nobody feeds them, but they live out in the woods. When it is cold, they don't come and lie down by the fire; but they are not badly off for all that. They scratch and scratch till they have made a hole deep in the ground, and they can run in there and be quite warm and comfortable with their little ones. That was what the text said—'The foxes have——?'"

"Holes!"

"Well done, Mary. Say that all together—'The foxes have holes.' Bella can tell me what flies in the air and sings! Bella wasn't listening—what a pity! Bella, Sophy will have to tell me. What is it, Sophy?"

"Birds, teacher."

"Bella is listening now, so she shall answer the next. What do the little birds live in, Bella?"

"Holes, teacher."

("Hush, Hetty!") No, Bella, it is the foxes that live in holes. But what do the little birds build in the hedges and up in the trees? You know! What the naughty boys take?"

"Nesses, teacher."

"That's it, Bella, nests. Nice, little, cosy nests, all lined with bits of wool and feathers to keep the little young birds warm, much better than we could make. And God taught them how to make them, so no wonder. So the foxes have"——

"Holes."

"And the birds of the air have "——

"Nests."

"And what have you got?"

No answer, so Bruey tried again.

"When it gets late, you don't get into a hole scratched in the ground, do you, like the foxes?"

"No, teacher!" "I gets into bed," added Hetty.

"To be sure! and that's warmer than the holes, and safer than the nests. You are better off than the foxes and birds. You have all got beds to lie down in when you are tired and sleepy, and when it is dark and cold and wet. But Jesus was not so well off as you. Not so well off as the foxes! For when He was very tired, and it was dark night, He had not anywhere at all to go. No house, and no bed! Only think! Jesus had not anywhere to lay His head. Say it—'The Son of Man' (that means Jesus) 'had not where to lay His head.'"

"I'd have given Him my pillow," Hetty said.

"There's on'y the bolster on our bed," Sophy remarked, as if she were considering what could be done.

"I should have liked to have given Him mine," Bruey answered, "because He must have been so very tired when He had been going about all day doing people all sorts of good. And because it was so kind of Him to come at all! He did not need to have come; He could have stayed up in heaven with the beautiful angels; but He came—why, Sophy, that's just what one of our texts is about—what Jesus came for—'Christ'"——And the children eagerly finished it.

"Yes, Christ Jesus came to save sinners, that means"——

"Naughty!"

"Yes, naughty people, and naughty little children, like us; else we must have been sent to that dreadful place to be punished. But Jesus came to save us from that; wasn't it good of Him! He stopped ever so many years down among wicked people on earth, and ever so often He was hungry and tired; and all the while He 'had not where to lay His head'; and you know how they killed Him at last, and nailed Him on the cross; and He let them do it, because He wanted to save us. What made Him take all that trouble for us? Nobody else ever did so much for us. What made Him do it?"

No answer; but Bruey was speaking as if it was a very real thing, and not just a story; and even Hetty looked serious.

"I know why, and I'll tell you. It was because He loved us so very much— loved us, oh, so dearly. Don't you recollect the text about it?"

"'We love Him'"——began Mary.

"'Because He first loved us,'" chimed in all the rest.

"Now we shall soon know the text. 'The foxes have'"——

"'Holes.'"

"'And the birds of the air'"——

"'Have nests.'"

"'But the Son of'"——

Only Hetty could supply the next word "Man."

"'Hath not where to'"——

"'Lay His head.'"

Still it took some time, and many trials, before all could say it right off. When even Bella had got through it without a mistake, Bruey said,

"Now, only think, we know five texts now—a whole handful, one for every finger!" And holding up her hand, and bidding the children do the same, a text was said for each finger, to their great delight. "We must try to get the other hand full soon. But now, who wants to hear what was the next thing Jesus did, after He made the poor leper well?"

Out went all the hands at once, Sophy also answering, "Me, teacher"; for which she received a poke from Hetty, who prided herself much on having remembered to answer by hand instead of tongue.

Bruey had begun telling them all she thought they could understand in St. Matthew's Gospel, carefully looking over beforehand, so that she might forget nothing. This Sunday, she told them about the good officer that asked Jesus to make his servant well, and about Peter's wife's mother getting well all at once when He only touched her hand; and then about a man that thought he would like to go about with Him, but did not think how poor Jesus was; and here the attention was beginning to flag a little, for perhaps Bruey was telling them too much at once; and Sophy was gaping.

"See if you can guess what is coming. The Lord Jesus wanted to see if the man really cared to go with Him, even if he would be very badly off, and so He said something to show him how poor He was. Guess what He said? Something that you can say?"

Sophy stopped gaping, and Hetty left off twisting the button of her jacket. But it was too difficult for them.

"Jesus wanted to show the man that He was so poor that He had not even any bed. Now, what did He say?"

Sophy brightened up—she had caught the idea; as soon as she began the text the others joined in, right pleased at finding a use so soon for the very text they had just learnt.

After this, they had sat quite long enough, so "Stand" was ordered again, and this time it was to learn a verse of a hymn begun the Sunday before. Bruey had a very large-type book, with a few hymns for children, in such large letters that all four little girls could see at once as she held the book in front of them, and pointed to each word. They could not read, but that did not matter. They just knew their letters, and could tell a very few of the commonest little words of two or three letters, so it was accounted great promotion to be shown quite long words all at once, and having something to *look* at made a variety. So the little eyes followed Bruey's pencil as she pointed to

> "There's a Friend for little children,
>   Above the bright blue sky;
> A Friend who never changeth,
>   Whose love can never die."

Only one line at a time though, till they nearly knew that, and then another. No spelling, that was weekday work; but sight and sound helped each other; and Hetty, especially, thought it a most delightful kind of reading to say word after word after Miss Bruey, and her triumph was great that she could tell "Friend" when it came again in the third line. They could "read" four lines quite fluently to their own satisfaction, which meant knowing them by heart, when the bell rang to close school.

There was no talking allowed, but Bruey heard Hetty say to Sophy—
"Our Alice says she shan't come with me this afternoon."

Afternoon came, and at ten minutes to three Bruey was at her post. Mary was before her, with a face considerably less wobegone than in the morning.

"Well, Mary, mother did not beat you, did she?"

"No, teacher. Her said if I liked to tear him, her shouldn't trouble herself about him. And Emma Fayling said her'd mend him for me to-morrow night, if I'd bring him."

"Then it will be all right, won't it? And you will mind next time you run by the boarding, won't you? Mary, I think the Lord Jesus did just what we asked Him this morning."

"Yes, teacher," answered Mary; but it was not intelligently said, and it was plain that she had not put two and two together. How many times every Sunday children say, "Yes, teacher," only because it is more likely to be all right than "No, teacher!"

"What did we ask Him, Mary?"

"Yes, teacher," would not do this time, so Mary had to think.

Bruey went on.

"We asked Him first for you not to feel so "——

"Sorry," supplied Mary.

"And don't you recollect you felt better directly, and you did not look at all sorry while we were learning the text and hymn; and I don't think you felt sorry and troubled again all the morning? You did not cry any more, did you?"

"No, teacher."

"Then, you see, the Lord Jesus did take away the trouble; how kind of Him! What else did we ask?"

"For mother not to beat me."

"And she did not?"

"No, teacher."

"Well, I'm quite sure that was because Jesus heard us ask Him, and so He kept mother from being angry with you. That was *two* kind things He did for you. But I think He did another. I think He put it into Emma's mind to mend your frock for you. And we had not asked Him about getting the frock mended. So this was more than we asked. Don't you think it was very good of Him, Mary?"

"Yes, teacher."

"Next time anything is the matter, you tell Him all about it again. It's better than telling anybody else. Why, Hetty, what is wrong?"

For Hetty had come up so quietly, that no one had heard her, and sat looking as dismal as if everything was wrong.

"Willie's a-crying, teacher. And it's all our Alice."

Not a very clear reason, thought Bruey, and not likely to be very serious.

"I daresay he will be smiling instead of crying by the time you get back, Hetty, so I wouldn't trouble about it."

"No, teacher, he won't; he'll fret ever so now. Alice has been and spent all her money, and Willie can't have no paint-box."

"But I thought Willie did not know."

"Please, teacher, Willie said a little bird told him, and I'm sure *I* didn't tell anybody except—except Charlie Dawler, and he said he wouldn't tell. But Willie took on ever so about it, 'cause Alice won't get no more money for a good bit."

"But perhaps Alice was obliged to spend her money on something else, and Willie won't be sorry when he finds it is for something better."

"No, teacher; Alice went out last night with some big girls, and she got a beautiful rose to put in her hat, just like yours, teacher, and she pinned it on after she came from church, and she's going a walk along with the big girls, instead of coming to school."

Bruey did not know how to soothe Hetty, who was full of sympathy and trouble for Willie, and of indignation against Alice for disappointing him. What could she say? Those words, "Just like yours, teacher," stopped her.

The second class teacher, Miss Anstey, stepped across, and, after a word to Bruey, said, "Hetty, is not your sister coming this afternoon?"

"No, teacher," replied Hetty, somewhat comforted by the fact of having something to communicate; "she's gone a walk with Lizzie Telf."

"Tell her I want to speak to her after church to-night; I will wait for her at the side door."

"Please, teacher, she isn't coming to-night; she told mother she shouldn't sit with the girls to-night; she should go to Lizzie Telf's church and sit in the gallery."

"I am sorry to hear that," said Miss Anstey, gravely, And she added, speaking to Bruey, "I am afraid there is no good reason for this. Hetty, you ask her to come with you, and not go with Lizzie Telf."

"Please, teacher, she won't be back to tea, and she won't sit with the girls at our church, 'cause she'd have to unpin the roses out of her hat."

But the bell rang and saved any further discussion. Miss Anstey went quickly to her seat, and Bruey looked very serious.

"That's the only good I see in your going, Bruey," said Percy, as they sat down to tea; "one can get something out of you at tea-time, after your labours. Now, tell us all about it." For Bruey's little accounts of her proceedings seemed to have a curious fascination for Percy, though Bruey could hardly tell whether he was not laughing at her all the time; but if he was, it was not the sort of "laughing at" that she minded, so it came to be quite an institution that she should tell all she chose of what had passed at school, and what her children had said and done. What she said to them, however, always remained a mystery; she could not retail that to any one.

"Come, we are not quite in such good spirits as usual; have you had to expel anybody? what's spoilt it, Bruey?"

Bruey could not have explained the real reason of what Percy was so quick to see. However, there was another.

"I have had two new ones put into my class; Miss Allison brought them to me directly after prayers this afternoon, and it is not so nice as having only my own."

"But they are to be your own, too, are they not?"

"Yes; but it's not like the same. They don't know what Hetty calls the 'back texts and hymns,' and it makes such a long line, six of them. I can't manage half so well, because I can't look at both ends of the form at once, and they are sure to play if one isn't always looking at them."

"Then I should put the worst ones in the middle, and the good ones outside."

"That is just what I do; but then it is rather hard upon the good ones; they don't like being outside."

"I daresay Miss Allison would manage for you to have another short form, Bruey," said Mrs. Murray; "and you could put them slantwise to each other, like a V; then all would be near to you, and you could see them all at once better."

"So I could! Oh, I hope she will! I always thought it would be so much nicer to have the children all round you, like the big classes. But I had so few till now."

"I found it so when I had a class," continued Mrs. Murray. "The forms used to be set so as to make great wide classes, so that one's own children were sitting quite scattered and far off from the teacher's chair, and yet close back to back to the adjoining classes. And nobody had the sense to move the forms a little, so as to make nice compact classes, with a good space between each."

"My children always seem to like to get near me, especially when I am telling them anything. And I do not have to speak so loud, either; they often listen best when I am speaking most softly. They lean forward, and think it is something very particular, if I speak quite low." Then Bruey recounted Hetty's description of Willie. "And, Percy, I thought you would lend me that magazine that your papa sends you. You don't want them, do you?"

"Yes, I do; I was going to have them bound at the end of the year."

"Well, then, if I put a paper cover outside, and lent them to Willie, and told him to take care of them, they would do to bind all the same. It is not as if they were bound already. You won't mind, will you?"

"No, I don't mind. Only, if you lend him one at a time, he is not so likely to spoil them."

"I want you to do something else for me, Percy; but I won't ask you two things at once."

"Nonsense; don't you see I am in a very gracious mood! I might be very ungracious next time, so 'make hay while the sun shines.'"

"I was thinking—you can write and draw so nicely, and if you would draw me a text in some sort of large open letters, like you did my name on the cover of my copy-book, Willie could paint them."

"What next, Bruey! So we give illumination lessons, do we?"

Bruey seldom took any notice of Percy's banter when her mind was possessed with an idea.

"Mamma, might I tear a leaf or two out of my drawing-book? Or would you find me some rather stiff paper?"

"Was ever a fellow so put upon!" bemoaned Percy. "You will have to guide my hand, Bruey; how can I tell what will please your Serene Highness? And how am I to find time for this sort of occupation?"

"I don't mean anything grand. I only want what you could do in about five minutes; it would not matter about doing it very beautifully, and quite plain letters would do; so that it was what he could colour with his blue and red paint, and perhaps a little ink."

"I suppose I must try. Victimised, as usual! What text do you want?"

"I thought you would choose one or two after tea; you ought to know what a boy would like better than I."

So, after tea, Percy found himself engaged in a new occupation, rummaging in the Bible, which Bruey took care to bring him at once, for texts to pencil out for this cripple boy.

"Could you look out about half-a-dozen, Percy, such as you think would look nice in large letters, and then let me choose?"

When she came down with her things on for evening service, Percy was still at work.

"Here! I'm sure I don't know which of these will do." And he tossed her a paper with several short texts scribbled on it; while he put the last stroke to one which he had pencilled out in large letters on a sheet of writing paper. It was— "Thou God seest me." "I shall not do another with a G in it, it is such a horrid letter to do. I wanted one with a capital W, but I could not see anything except 'Wine is a mocker,' and I thought this was more your style of thing. I looked in Proverbs mostly: lots of short texts there."

"This will do famously; it is just what I meant." She took it up.

"Oh, that is only just to try, on common paper; leave that!"

"Then it will do all the better for Willie to try on; please don't tear it up, he can go on with this one till you can do another or two for him. What a good boy you are, Percy; it is so kind of you."

"Don't see that I had much choice about it! When a fellow has got to do a thing, he may as well do it first as last, and be done with it."

Ungracious words enough on paper, but though accompanied by a most injured look and tone, Bruey knew perfectly well what they meant, and was delighted accordingly.

Perhaps if Percy began doing little things for others for her sake, he might go on after a while to do them, and much more too, for higher and better motives.

CHAPTER III.

WORK NEARER HOME.

ON Monday morning Bruey stood brushing her hair in the dressing-room. The door between the two rooms stood open. Mrs. Murray was mending a frock which had received some slight damage in a battle with Percy on Saturday evening, respecting Bruey's departure to bed, of which Percy by no means approved. There had been no great hurry, and Mrs. Murray had not objected to ten minutes' play, Bruey's efforts to escape not being serious enough to put an end to what she enjoyed very much, till "O Percy, you have torn my gathers," made a truce expedient.

"Mamma, when am I to have a new hat?"

Mrs. Murray was rather surprised at the question: it was not a usual topic.

"Why do you want a new one! It is a very little while since Aunt Joseph gave you your best one, only when Percy came; and it is not like a dark, heavy, winter one. You certainly will not want anything done to it till quite summer, much less a new one."

Bruey meditated.

"What made you ask that?" asked Mrs. Murray, presently.

"Mamma, would you mind?—might I try?—I almost think I could—(if I might have a little velvet)—just trim it up fresh."

"My dear child, what can you want to spoil that nice hat for?" She was puzzled, both at the request and at Bruey's hesitating manner.

Bruey laid down her brush and came forward.

"I had better tell you exactly all about it, mamma. Miss Allison said something to me yesterday morning about its being a rule for the children not to wear flowers, and that it was better for the teachers to keep it too, else it made the children want to wear them."

"Well?"

"And so I thought, if you did not mind, I could take the flowers off my hat myself, and you would give me a bit of velvet (it wouldn't want much), just for the front."

Mrs. Murray did not look quite pleased. "I think it is a great pity any fuss is made about such things. Children ought to learn that there is difference of station, and that they must not expect to see ladies dressing like themselves. I know a great many good people think differently, but I cannot say that I see it myself."

Bruey was terribly perplexed. She was sure her mother was always right, and could not admit the idea that she could possibly be wrong. And yet she had a strong feeling that though it might not be *wrong* to wear flowers, yet that it would be *right* not to wear them. She could not put the difference into words, but she felt it. Besides, her mother had not heard all Miss Allison said, and these school children might be different from those which her mother had known. She had a most uncomfortable feeling about Alice Fosbery, and Hetty's words, "Just like yours, teacher," haunted her, and made her feel still more uncomfortable. But she could not tell her mother about this, for what was there to tell? She did not know that Alice's roses had anything to do with hers; and Alice might have got them all the same, and stayed away from school to wear them just the same, if Bruey had had the plainest hat in all Rilverton.

"But, you see, it's a rule, mamma."

"Yes, dear, for the children, but not for the teachers."

"Miss Allison seemed to think it came to that."

"Here is your frock, Bruey."

"Oh, thank you, mamma." She took it and put it on, not seeing how to go on with the conversation. She went back into the dressing-room, shutting the door, as she always did, and curled herself up on her box to read her chapter. She was reading straight through Chronicles in the morning; it was very interesting, for she did not hear these chapters read in church, as so many in Kings were. When she had read her chapter, she always took a pencil, kept on purpose in the little table drawer, and marked a verse. It often took her a good while to choose what she thought would be the very nicest, but it helped her wonderfully to remember not only where the favourite verses came, but the whole chapter. Nearly always she knelt down with her Bible open, and turned the marked verse into a prayer. If she did not, it was more often because she was hurried and careless, than because there was nothing in the chapter which she could turn into prayer.

This morning it was the thirteenth chapter of the second book of Chronicles. She thought the last part the most interesting—the story of the ambush and the trumpets and the shout; and the eighteenth verse seemed a nice one to mark—"*The children of Judah prevailed, because they relied upon the Lord God of their fathers.*" But she would look once more over the chapter. "I wonder I did not notice that!" was her thought as she lighted on part of the eleventh verse—"*We keep the charge of the Lord our God.*" "That meant attending to the sacrifices and incense and golden candlesticks for the priests and Levites. I wonder if it means Sunday-school for me!" Yes, she supposed it must, for her little girls had been given her as a charge; and it was very grand and solemn to think that it was not just Miss Allison's charge, but "*the charge of the Lord our God.*" It would not be hard to turn this into a prayer, for she did want to keep this charge, and she hardly knew how much that meant, and she would like not to leave anything undone; and so she must pray to be shown how to keep it, and then to be helped always to keep it. Had this hat business anything to do with it? She was not quite clear, but was inclined to think it had. For it would not be keeping her charge if she did anything, as Miss Allison said, which might possibly help to "hinder any little girl from thinking of her soul and her Saviour," even if it were a girl in another class. But what if her mamma thought differently, and did not allow her to untrim her hat? Well, she would wait and see. And, meanwhile, she knelt down and prayed that she might keep the charge of the Lord her God, and that she might be helped to do just what was right about the hat.

She went downstairs.

Mrs. Fayling was cleaning the door-steps. Mrs. Murray's housemaid was a delicate girl, but so valuable in some respects that she preferred having a woman to help now and then to sending her away altogether.

"Good morning, Mrs. Fayling. How is old Mrs. Fayling?"

"Thank you, miss; she's pretty well for her."

"Did Bella say her text to her yesterday?"

"Well, miss, her Grannie asked her, and she did try, but she isn't very bright, miss, and I don't think she gives much heed. 'The foxes has nesses,' was all she could say. Grannie quite looks for her texts now, but she never can say the fresh one."

"Then, she can recollect the old ones?"

"Yes, miss; she always knows the back ones, and can say them quite pretty to Grannie. She'll know this one next Sunday, but we could not make top nor tail of it yesterday. That little girl of Mrs. Fosbery's next door comes in and says them too, quite pleased like. Grannie misses her sight so badly, and now Emma goes to work, there's no one to read to her, except when your mamma is good enough to come, so it's quite an amusement to the old lady to hear the texts."

"Mrs. Fayling, hasn't Mrs. Fosbery a cripple boy?"

"Yes, miss, a poor, fretchit little fellow. Times he'll take on about anything, and sit there and whine by the hour. Yesterday you could have heard him fret, fret, fret, all the afternoon."

"What was the matter?" asked Bruey, eagerly.

"I don't rightly know; it don't take much to make him take on. Mrs. Fosbery said it was because he thought Alice was going to get him something he'd set his head on, and then she went out Saturday night and bought a flower with the money, to stick in her hat. Mrs Fosbery said she said her mother ought to like it, because it was just like yours, Miss Bruey. 'Just like her impudence!' says I; and I should have given her my mind about it, but she never came home till near nine o'clock at night. Girls is that foolish! and if once they take to buying finery and rubbish, to show off on Sundays, they come to no good."

"Bruey, don't stand at the door any longer; you will catch cold."

She turned; her mother was close by just inside the dining-room door. She had not heard her come down.

The bell rang.

"Prayer-time, and Percy not down again!" said Mrs, Murray. "It will not do to go on this way."

They did not wait; it was no new thing; and Percy could not be in time for school if they did.

"Go and call that boy," she said, after prayers.

Bruey went up and knocked at his door.

"Percy, we have had prayers."

"That's all right," was the reply from within. "Get on with your breakfast, Bruey; I'll undertake to catch you,—shall be down in three minutes."

"You do not deserve any breakfast," said his aunt, rather shortly, when he made his appearance.

"Very sorry, Aunt—beg pardon—promise not to be late again, till to-morrow morning."

Mrs. Murray showed her displeasure by not vouchsafing another word. Bruey felt it was not quite right to talk and laugh with Percy when her mamma was vexed with him. And as Percy had to eat in good earnest to make up for lost time, there was very little said till he finished his coffee, and set down the cup with a clatter.

"Excuse me, Aunt; I must run for it."

Her assent was silent. Bruey followed him out of the room.

"Have you got everything Percy, or can I fetch you anything?"

"No, I'm all right. Stay, no; there's my knife, it's in the top drawer—look sharp, Bruey!"

Bruey ran upstairs, found the knife, and came down panting.

"The magazines are there," she said; "may I take the January one for Willie Fosbery?"

"Yes, yes; only don't hinder me." And he scampered off.

"Bruey!"

"Yes, Mamma."

"I shall not be ready to sit down till about half past ten; but you have plenty to do; practise first, and then go on with your French translation, and write out 'savoir.' You may look over it before you begin, and then shut the book, and write it from memory."

Bruey looked at the little clock on the mantelpiece—it was five minutes to nine. She would just warm her hands and feet, and begin at nine.

She practised her half-hour. Her mamma came in and out two or three times, making an occasional remark in passing.

"Mind that G sharp, dear. That variation wants playing quite ten times extra, Bruey."

But after half-past nine, when Bruey sat down at her little desk, the door was not opened again. She began her French translation. It was a pretty little story, but this morning she had come to a dull bit—some moral reflections at the beginning of a new chapter, in two long paragraphs. It was so much nicer to do when it was conversation in very short paragraphs, and did not seem to take so long. Two unknown words in the very first clause to be looked out, and *then* it did not seem to make sense. She yawned. "I must put down the words as they come, and ask mamma what it means. I know all the words, but, oh, dear! I suppose it is an *idiom*. I wish there were no idioms. I hope there won't be any more down this page." The next sentence came easy, but the next was hard again.

A sound of small wheels came near the window, and she looked up to see what was coming. It was a truck with some furniture on it. "Sure to be for the end house," thought Bruey. "I wonder who has taken it." She got up and went to the window to watch it to the end of the terrace, seven or eight houses off. And then she could just see two men unloading it. "But I *must* go on with my translation." She sat down, but the third sentence was quite as awkward as the first. "I wish it was exercise-morning instead of translation-morning," sighed Bruey. The clock gave warning. "Ten minutes to ten! Oh, dear! Perhaps if I did my verb first, I could do this better afterwards." She pushed away the translation books, and opened a grammar, over which she leant with her forehead on her hands, and her elbows on the table. "*Je sais, tu sais, il sait. Nous savons, vous savez*—Miss Anstey said that to Miss Winter coming home yesterday; what was she talking about? I wish I might walk home by myself; it can't matter. I wish Miss Allison went home my way. I wonder if I shall ever be a superintendent. I should not like giving addresses. But I should like keeping the books. I think I should have different marks, more like what mamma gives me." And Bruey soon made out a neat little scheme of marks, and tried them on her slate to see how they would look, and fancied herself explaining them to the teachers. *Ten!* The sound brought her back from her superintendentship. "Where did I leave off? I had read the preterite, had I not? I rather wish I had finished the translation first, but I have lost the place now, so I had better go on with this." She read to the end of the verb, and was rubbing out the marks on her slate, in order to write it, when wheels again came near. Another truck, this time carrying a piano, not very securely placed. She must just watch that—only for a minute; it looked just as if it were going to topple over. However, it reached the end house safely.

She came back to her verb rather conscience-smitten. She wished she had not gone twice to the window, and there had been nothing very particular to see after all.

She closed her grammar, as her mamma told her to do, and began to write "*savoir.*" She got on flourishingly through the present, and the imperfect was always easy after she once knew the *a, i, e, n, t,* which ran off so naturally on the five fingers. But what *was* the preterite? She could not recollect in the least. She tried "*Je savai, tu savas,*" but that was evidently wrong. If she was obliged to look, she must rub out what she had written and begin again, for she was not allowed to refer to the book again after beginning the verb. What a tiresome thing! She would try to recollect without. She wrote *Je sav*—in large letters. "It *must* begin that way." Then she touched up the letters with double strokes. It looked well. Willie Fosbery could paint letters like that: if Percy could not be persuaded to trace any more, she would try herself. Whereupon she made a large S, then saw that it could be improved upon, and made another. But oh, dear! *Je* what? It would be the shortest way, after all, to read the verb again, and then write it straight off, and she wished she had done that at once.

She took the book, and found "*savoir.*" "Preterite, *Je sus!* I could not have noticed that at all. I don't believe I read it. Why *do* the French have such irregular verbs?"

Soon after half-past ten Mrs. Murray came in with a work-basket. Bruey started. "Oh, Mamma, I did not know it was so late."

"What are you doing? Imperative, I see. Finish the verb. I would always rather you did less translation, so as to get the whole verb written."

Bruey did finish it, feeling anything but happy.

"Here it is, Mamma."

"You have missed out the conditional altogether; this won't do. No! you have written the plural of the conditional under the future. How could you be so careless? And see here, actually a mistake in the imperfect! Now, the translation."

"Mamma, I'm very sorry. I don't know how it was. I couldn't make sense; it's such a stupid piece."

Mrs. Murray saw at a glance the state of things. Not five lines done, instead of a page.

She did not say much, but what she did, stung Bruey terribly.

"If this is what comes of going to the Sunday-school, the sooner you give up that the better. I suppose I must come and sit by you all the time, as you can't be trusted. Now, get your history."

"It was some furniture going to the end house that I got up to see," said Bruey, with a faint hope that her mother's curiosity might be excited.

No answer.

"I did not mean to idle, Mamma. I really couldn't make the translation out."

No answer; and it was plain there would be none, and this was worse than a scolding. Mrs. Murray worked in perfect silence while Bruey read her history aloud—not a question, nor an explanation.

When that was over, Mrs. Murray gave her a share of the mending to do.

"You can't make a mistake; it is all pinned ready."

After a while, Bruey tried a query.

"Are you going out this morning, Mamma!"

"I don't know."

Another interval.

"Mamma, do you know where Farr's Court is? One of my children lives there."

"Never heard of it."

Another interval.

"Mamma, is this to be felled?"

"Of course."

A tear fell on Bruey's work.

"I would rather be scolded, ten to one. And I'm tired. Everything's wrong to-day. I thought it would have been such a good opportunity to ask Mamma lots of things—about Mary Shelton's frock, and my plans for Willie, and about Percy. And I thought she would have let me go with her to her district, but she won't even tell me whether she is going out at all. I wish she would take some notice of me."

They worked on; the clock ticked as usual, but surely the hand did not move at its usual rate; would it never be twelve o'clock?

A footstep sounded on the gravel, and then on the doorsteps. A knock and ring.

"Who can that be so early? I wish people would keep to afternoon calls, and not come at all hours," said Mrs. Murray.

Jane tapped at the door, and handed a card to her mistress.

"She asked for you first, ma'am, and then if Miss Bruey was in."

"Who is it, Mamma?"

Mrs. Murray left the room, saying—

"Finish that bit, Bruey, and then you can come into the drawing-room."

"Who is it, Jane?"

"I did not notice the name, Miss; but it's a lady—not a young lady."

Bruey yawned, and wished she need not go. She finished the few stitches, and then went upstairs to smooth her hair. There would be the less time to sit in state.

But it was Miss Allison! Bruey forgot her troubles as she opened the drawing-room door and saw who it was. Miss Allison kissed her, and told her, in a few words, what she had been telling her mother at greater length, that she called on her way to the end house, where she would be busy all day.

"For we are coming to live there; so before next Sunday we hope to be your near neighbours."

Bruey coloured with pleasure: Miss Allison actually going to live so near! How nice!

"I have been telling your mamma, dear, that, if she has no objection, I should like you to see the *Sunday School Magazine* regularly, and that was why I called at once, otherwise you would miss the last number, which I meant to have given you yesterday afternoon, but Miss Denton forgot to bring it back."

"Thank you very much," said Bruey, who felt rather exalted at this implied recognition of her position as a teacher.

"See, there is a list of names pasted inside, with the date to each. I give it to the first class teacher on the first Sunday in the month; she brings it back next Sunday, and gives it to the second class teacher, and so on till it reaches the eighth class. Then the eighth class teacher will give it to you, and you will keep it the week, and bring it back to me next Sunday. So the one copy does very good service, does it not?"

"Am I to bring it to you at school, or leave it at your house?"

"Bring it back to school, please, because I let some of the first class girls have the old copies; it gives them some idea how to teach, if I want them to take a little class when a teacher is unexpectedly away."

"But most of the teachers only teach once in the day," said Mrs. Murray, "so it must take a long time to go all round."

"I keep two copies going, one for the morning and the other for the afternoon teachers, so there is never any difficulty about passing it on. It is much easier to get it done regularly by putting the dates beforehand; a teacher does not like to keep it till the 17th, when the book shows that she ought to have brought it on the 10th. I find, too, that they read them much more certainly than when lent for an indefinite time, or given outright; when 'any time will do,' they are put aside for other things, and often never read at all."

"I am sure Bruey will like to read it very much," said Mrs. Murray; "it is good of you to think of her as a teacher."

"I hope to have a little talk with Bruey some day, but I must not stay now, or I shall find the sideboard in the drawing-room, and the chests of drawers in the dining-room. Perhaps we can walk home from school together some Sunday." And she looked affectionately at Bruey.

"I *should* like it," said Bruey, warmly.

"I do not know about continuing afternoon school," Mrs. Murray said. "We must see that Sunday work does not interfere with Monday's work. It will not do for lessons to be half done in consequence."

Miss Allison never needed much explanation. She knew pretty well what it was to feel unaccountably out of sorts on a Monday morning, and how the Enemy tempts people who have overtired themselves to be naughty in all sorts of ways.

"Bruey will try to do herself on Monday all she tells her little girls to do on Sunday, won't you, Bruey? I think all the work we try to do for others shows us how much work there is to do for ourselves. But I *must* go."

And she went away. Bruey watched her, and wondered what had passed before she came in; and whether Miss Allison had said anything about her hat; and whether her mother had said anything else about herself. She wished she had gone in at once; her hair had not been so very untidy after all.

"Put on your things, Bruey, and go out in the garden. But come and put your books and work away first."

She did as she was bid. Before she had been many minutes in the garden, she saw her mamma come out and go towards the town. She had her bag in her hand, which might mean either shopping or tracts. It meant tracts, however, *this* time, Bruey was sure, because she had seen the brown paper covers peeping out as the bag lay half open on the hall table when she came out. And tracts meant going to Gilling's Yard, where the Fosberys lived, and where she had hoped to go. Willie would get no magazine and no text to paint this week!

There was one hope—Mrs. Murray had little more than an hour before dinner, and she might possibly go again in the afternoon to finish her round. But everything was wrong to-day; so where was the use of supposing this?

Bruey sauntered about the garden, picked some violets for a little vase, and finally got up into a tree, to continue certain experiments as to which boughs were particularly good for swinging on. Do not be shocked; Bruey made up for her bad running by excellent climbing; and though she was just getting old enough to have misgivings about its being quite the most ladylike performance in the world, she could not yet refrain from her pet amusement. What it would be like to be quite too old for it, and to be reduced to walking on gravel and grass, when she was sent out into the garden, was too dismal to think about. She forgot the clouds for a little while, but soon got tired of her gymnastics, and then they came back.

"I wish I need not stay out till one o'clock. I wish Percy would come home. I wish I could have gone to Willie Fosbery. I wish we had a tree like that mulberry in the next garden. I wish—well, I wonder why I don't feel good like I did last night and this morning. I ought not to have idled, I know, but it was such a horrid piece of French. But I wish I had not idled. Was it *really* wrong? Sin? What made me think of that? Such a little thing can't be sin, can it? Oh, I *wish* I hadn't! I think I'll go upstairs and pray about it when I go in; perhaps I shall feel better if I do. There's Percy!" And she went to meet him.

"Everything's wrong to-day!" said he. ("Just what I said!" thought Bruey.) "I believe they put the school-clock on, on purpose,—it's been two minutes slow for a week, and now I'll declare it's two minutes fast. So how was a fellow likely to be in time?"

"You were late, then?"

"Yes, and got a vile imposition."

"Come and have a climb," said Bruey.

"No, I shan't; I'm going to get this done before school if I can, else I should have to do it after, and I've other fish to fry then."

And Percy disappeared into the house. It was nearly one o'clock, so Bruey soon followed him. But she was not inclined to pray now. The drawer into which she put her gloves was slightly disarranged, and Bruey was a very tidy little body, so she put it all to rights, arranging the different articles on a new plan which she thought an improvement.

"There will be plenty of time; Mamma is not come in yet." Then she took up a necktie, and twisted it. "I could do my hat with something like this, I do believe." She next got the hat itself in a dawdling sort of way, and tried the effect of a large bow, then of a fold. She put it on the dressing-table, and thereby upset a box of pins. These had to be picked up, and then she might as well stick a fresh supply into the pincushion; and who was to resist doing this in a pattern? Mrs. Murray's step and voice were heard.

"Come and find me a handkerchief, Bruey. I have been delayed, and we shall hardly have done dinner in time for Percy."

So the good moment was over, and Bruey went down to dinner with the cloud still upon her, which prayer might have taken away.

After dinner came visitors, and after that practising and lessons to prepare for next day, and after that came Percy and tea-time. After that, twilight. Should she go upstairs till the gas was lighted? She lingered at the window.

"Bruey, let us have a game at dominoes till Jane lights the gas. I must get to work then; but we shall have time for a game or two." The opportunity was lost, and she sat down to the game. They played till the gas was lighted, and then Percy had other wants. Could not Bruey just look him out some words in his Latin lexicon? And then just see if he could repeat a lesson or two. He liked having a home fag. So the time passed till it was too late to be worth while to go upstairs.

"Now, Bruey, I think you might unpick this sleeve for me," said Mrs. Murray. "Take off the trimming, and undo the seam as far as that pin; no farther."

Bruey took it, not very graciously. It always went against her when her mamma said, "I think you might do so and so," though she could not have told why. She lounged and gaped.

"O Bruey, you careless child, see what work you have given me! I had better have done it myself."

For she had unpicked as far as the pin, sure enough, but from the wrong end of the seam.

She sighed. "You said as far as the pin." It was a sulky, half-impertinent tone. Mrs. Murray gave her no answer but a look, and went on unpicking. "Mamma, I can finish it."

"Leave it to me, my dear." And there was nothing for it but to watch her mother do it, and stitch up again what was unpicked by mistake.

"That's a deliverance!" said Percy, pushing his books away in a heap. "Now, I can draw one of those texts you wanted, and you will put my books up, won't you?" She was quite alive now, as busy and bright as possible.

In ten minutes Mrs. Murray said, "It is quite time you said good-night, Bruey; Percy can do that quite well without you, and you are very tired."

She knew the tone was hopelessly decided, so she said good-night, and went upstairs. Sat down and cried to begin with,—cried angrily at first. Mamma might have let her finish the seam, instead of doing it herself in that way.

Mamma might have let her stay and see Percy finish that one text; she was not always so particular. She did not feel inclined to do anything, neither to read her chapter nor to prepare for bed, certainly not to pray, so she went on crying, curled up on her box, with her arms and head on her table. A long string of wishes, some of them contradictory enough, passed through her mind, coming at last to this, "I wish I had not spoken so sulkily to mamma." Something fastened this wish upon her, and she wished it over and over again. Just then she started at a rattling knock at her door.

"Can you come here half a minute? I've done one text, and I want to know if you like it before I begin another."

She hastily wiped her eyes and opened the door, keeping in the shade, that Percy might not see she had been crying.

"Yes, it was very nice."

But Percy pushed the door wider open, and the light fell on her face.

"Hallo, Bruey! what now? You have been crying. You are not ill, are you?"

He spoke quite gently and sympathisingly. She began to cry again in consequence. Percy was troubled.

"Won't you tell me what's the matter?"

"O Percy, I've been so naughty. I wish I hadn't spoken so to mamma."

He whistled, and looked quite relieved.

"That's all, is it? I always thought you were a queer one. You naughty? Why, you are always as good as gold!"

"And I looked out of the window instead of doing my French this morning."

What made her say that? Was it a secret feeling that Percy would think her very good to be troubled about such a little thing as that?

"My dear cousin, do you suppose I *ever* do my Greek without looking out of the window? unless I'm grinding against time, that is. Well, girls *are* different from boys! I thought there was something quite awful the matter."

"Percy, don't go hindering Bruey now," called Mrs. Murray; "it is time she was in bed; come down."

"All right, Aunt." And he swung himself downstairs.

So Bruey was looking the picture of woe all about two things, which he was quite sure would never have troubled his conscience for a moment. Was it only because she was a girl and he a boy? Was she always so sorry about little faults? Was it possible that *he* might ever see them as seriously? He did not like this thought; if he did, how awful it would be, for surely Bruey's greatest sins would be less than his least, and he could recollect enough to make him feel that, if his sorrow were to be in proportion to hers, it would be something terrible indeed.

Meanwhile Bruey was more unhappy than ever. She knew now *why* she had said that to Percy, and she hated herself for it. To think that, instead of being really sorry for a sin, she had actually used it to make Percy think her wonderfully good! This brought the sin and wrong of the whole day home to her, and the tears were no longer angry ones, but penitent ones.

But the day had not been all bad. She had prayed quite earnestly in the morning. And yet she had been wrong all day. How was this? She had not watched. True enough, but was this all? She recollected her morning prayer, that she might *"keep the charge of the Lord her God,"* and how she was just a little bit lifted up with the grand idea, and had only her Sunday-school charge in her mind as she prayed. For she could not recollect that she had prayed at all about a charge nearer home—the little self over which she had to keep watch; she quite forgot to ask for any grace to make this little person industrious at her lessons, and careful at her work, and good-tempered and sweet all day, and full of happy love to the Lord Jesus. The Lord Jesus! That name made the sorrow deeper. She was really very sorry that she had vexed her mamma, but the Lord Jesus—that sweet name—had she not grieved Him more? For He had seen and known much more; He knew how she had been wandering in heart from Him all day, and had not once cared to come near to Him, even to ask Him for help and forgiveness, much less to tell Him how much she loved Him, and to seek to feel His love to her.

She was on her knees at last, trying to tell Him how sorry she was, and wishing He would send a sweet word of forgiveness to her, like that happy time in the autumn, which she never forgot. But no such blessed answer came. Though He forgives His children, and truly and surely receives them as soon as they return to Him after wandering away, yet He does not always let them know and feel this at once. Even little Christian children, like dear Bruey, have to learn, over and over again, that it is an evil and bitter thing to depart from the Lord, even if only for one day.

So, though she felt hushed when she had finished her prayer, she did not feel happy, but quietly sad.

She was not quite ready for bed when her mamma came upstairs.

"Not in bed? This won't do, Bruey; I did not send you upstairs to idle and dawdle."

Half-an-hour before, Bruey would have answered again, but now she only hastened her movements. Still it was rather trying; her good mother would have been only kind and glad if she had known how the time had been spent, but how could she tell her? Of course she could not, so she must bear the accusation. But she would like to say something, though it was always a terrible effort.

Her mamma came and tucked her up in a quick business-like way, and gave her a kiss to match—short and business-like. Bruey's intended speech was not made in time, and her mother left the room. And Bruey fell asleep.

It seemed as if she had been asleep a long time, when she woke and saw a light in the room, and her mother sitting bolt upright in her chair, as if startled. She did not know what woke her, but she had been dreaming that Sophy Willis brought the baby to school, and the baby had brought the bottle of cough mixture, and threw it down on the floor with such a noise that she woke just as she was wondering if she should give Sophy or the baby a bad mark.

She started up. "Mamma, what is it?"

"Hush! Listen!"

But there was no sound.

"I did not hear anything, Mamma?"

"I certainly heard *something*," said Mrs. Murray. "A sort of thump, like something falling."

Bruey was frightened.

"You don't think it's robbers, Mamma?"

"Robbers, no; I hope not! It's too early for that, only ten minutes past eleven. But I should like to know *what* it was, for the servants went to bed at ten, and Percy went at nine, and has been asleep this hour and a half. His gas was out when I came upstairs."

She rose and went to the door. Bruey jumped out of bed and followed her. As Mrs. Murray opened the door, she turned and said, "Get into bed, Bruey, you can't do any good," and then went out and listened on the landing. All was perfectly still and dark, the gas being all turned off except in her own room. She came back for a candle, and went downstairs. Bruey did get into bed, but could not stay there, as her mother did not immediately return. She crept again to the door, making no sound with her bare feet. She felt sure she heard a slight noise in Percy's room, which was on the other side of the landing. She went across, and listened at the door. "Percy!" But all was quiet. "Percy, are you asleep?" No sound, so she went back again. Mrs. Murray came upstairs. "It is all safe and quiet, Bruey, perhaps I was mistaken, and yet"——

"Mamma, I thought I heard a very little noise in Percy's room, and I went and listened, and called to him; but he must be asleep, for he did not answer. But—I don't know, perhaps it was fancy—but I thought I saw a light under his door just the first instant you opened your door."

"I saw none, Bruey."

"It was only for an instant, when you told me to go back to bed, and it was gone directly."

"That is not likely, or I think I should have seen it. But I will go and see."

Percy's door was fastened. Mrs. Murray did not like to wake him, and all seemed quiet; so she came back to her room, and in a few minutes was lying beside Bruey.

"Mamma, I will try and do my lessons well tomorrow."

"I hope you will; but it won't do for you to be so taken up with all sorts of other things as to be careless and naughty at home. I thought you wanted to be a Christian child in truth as well as in name, and set a good example to Percy; but I don't see all I should like to see."

"O Mamma!" began Bruey, very sorrowfully.

"There, that will do," said Mrs. Murray, kissing her, "you go to sleep now. I must not have any talking at this time of night."

CHAPTER IV.

FINDING WORK FOR WILLIE.

NEXT morning Bruey was again in her little room. Today must not be like yesterday.

She read her chapter, 2 Chronicles 14. The 11th verse, Asa's beautiful prayer, was a prayer all ready for her, so she would mark that, at any rate a part of it. "*Help us, O Lord our God.*" That would just do—the very words she wanted to say. But the pencil need not stop there. "*For we rest on Thee.*" She could not have put it into words, but this gave her a feeling of strength and peace, and sounded like quiet music. "*And in Thy name we go against this multitude.*" She was sure it was a multitude which she had to go against, for every day she found that she failed in something, and usually in exactly the very thing which she had forgotten to pray about. And she would have to go against some of this multitude to-day—temper, idleness, excuses, forgetfulness, some of them, perhaps all.

Her Bible lay open still, and after her prayer she glanced again at it, and her eye caught the pencil-mark in the thirteenth chapter: "*We keep the charge of the Lord our God.*" "Why, I forgot all about it this morning, and *only* prayed for myself. I wish I could remember to pray for my children every day." She knelt again, and asked God to bless them in a few words.

But she thought again about it while putting her room tidy before going down. What did "bless them" mean? Ever so much. And it meant rather different things too for each, as well as some which were the same for all. There would not be time to pray all that every day. Six of them, that was one for each day; she wondered she had not thought of this before. She took her pencil and made a neat little list on the back of a card.

Monday, . . . Hetty Fosbery.
Tuesday, . . . Mary Shelton.

Wednesday, . . Bella Fayling.
Thursday, . . Sophy Willis.
Friday, . . . Nanny Smith.
Saturday, . . . Betsy Barnett.

Now, there is only Sunday; perhaps there would be another new girl after a while; but stay! need she pray in this way only for them? There was Percy—poor, dear, good Percy—she did not like to think he was not a Christian, and yet he did not seem to care much for good things, and said he did not like Sunday; though in other respects Bruey thought him much better than herself. But if he did not really love Jesus, was not that as great a thing to pray for as her class? Surely it was. So she put down—

Sunday, ... P. M.

"That looks like 'afternoon,'" she thought, so if she should ever let her card fall out of her Bible, it would not matter if he picked it up. And she would indeed pray that Percy might learn to love Sunday, by learning to love the Lord Jesus.

Things went better than the day before as to herself, though Percy was late for breakfast again.

After lessons Mrs. Murray told her she might come down with her to Gilling's Yard. Delightful!

There were three texts to take to Willie, and the magazine. She went to Percy's drawer to find it—February, March—where was January? A wonderful confusion reigned in that drawer; so Bruey rummaged under and among its contents, finding the magazine at last under a tangled mass of fishing tackle. In the search she came upon two or three yellow books which she had not seen before. She looked into them; they were stories certainly, but quite grown-up ones, and not very attractive to her. She wondered if they were at all pretty, and carried one off to her own room to read.

When Bruey and her mamma reached Gilling's Yard, they saw the cripple Willie, with his poor little shrunken legs, in a tiny arm-chair, outside the door of his home. He looked like one of those comic pictures, all head and scarcely any body. There was brown hair falling over a great white forehead, which a skinny little hand swept back now and then. His eyes might have been beautiful for they were so large and dark, but for the sulky scowl of his brows. There was no colour on his lips, and they had a nervous twitch now and then. Altogether he was "a hobject," as the neighbours described him; and he had wits enough to know the fact, and feelings enough to be very sore about it. He had become used to seeing Mrs. Murray, or rather to her seeing him, which was a greater consideration; but if he had caught sight in time of the strange little lady who followed, he would have "hitched" himself out of sight with surprising quickness. However, Bruey happened to come up the yard behind her mamma, as the flagging was very narrow, so Willie did not spy her till Mrs. Murray spoke to him, and it was too late to escape.

"How are you, Willie?" she said.

"Quite as usual, ma'am," was the reply.

"My little daughter has brought something to amuse you. I daresay you are glad of something to do?"

"I have nothing to do."

"But you like to have something to do?"

"There is nothing I can do."

These answers were given in a cold, hopeless way, and though the voice was that of a little child, the tone and manner were more like a weary old man.

Bruey felt exceedingly sorry for him. She never saw before what a miserable thing life could seem with "nothing to do." How glad she was that she had something for him to do. Mrs. Murray went into the house, where Mrs. Fosbery was ironing, so she was left alone with him. It was much easier to begin by producing her texts than by talking.

"Look, Willie, do you think you could paint this?"

He looked eagerly, but did not speak.

"I thought you could do the capital letters red, and the rest blue; or how do you think it would look if you did the small letters black, with ink, you know, and just edge them with red?"

Willie took the offered text, evidently pleased.

"The capitals are beautiful," he said. "The small letters are very easy."

"Then you would like to paint them? You see one does not need a whole box of paints to do letters like these."

Willie looked up with an angry flash in his eyes.

"Hetty has been telling you!"

"Yes; Hetty told me all about you on Sunday."

"Hetty can't hold her tongue."

"But I think that is a very good thing, because if she had held her tongue I should not have known that you liked painting and reading."

Willie was silent. Bruey took another arrow from her quiver.

"And see, I have brought you a magazine to read." Again the eager look. "There are pictures, see, and something about animals, and such a pretty story about a boy who was a missionary, I am sure you will like that. You must tell me next time I come whether you liked it. And, Willie, my cousin and I often try to find out the answers to these Bible questions at the end; they are so curious sometimes. I thought if you would try too"——

She did not quite know how to go on. She wished Willie would talk.

"Have you got a Bible?"

"Oh, yes," he said, in a worried tone.

"Is it a nice one?"

"It's mother's."

"But I daresay she lets you have it?"

"When I want it. But I'm tired of it, the same as of all the other books. I have read all I care to. Samuel and Judges are interesting, but I don't like Psalms and Epistles."

"I wonder if you have read Chronicles? It is so interesting. I am reading that now, the stories about Abijah and Asa in the Second Book."

"I do not recollect those; where did you say they are?"

"In Chronicles. But, Willie, I think I like St. Luke and St. John better still."

Willie was getting interested. It was something quite new for any one to compare notes with him in this way.

"It's a long while since I read those. But I recollect a great deal in them. Isn't the story about the blind man and the clay in one of them? I liked that."

"Yes, that is in St. John, I think. I think all those stories about Jesus are the most beautiful of all. He was *so* good."

Bruey felt a little thrill of pleasure at having got thus far.

She felt she wished poor Willie knew more of Jesus than only the stories about Him, beautiful as they were. She did not suppose she should have been courageous enough to speak about Him, but the very mention of His Name, which had come so naturally, seemed to give her both happiness and strength. She would try to say a little more, though Willie had made no answer to her last remark.

"Willie, it's so nice to think that He is so kind, just like He was then, when He did all those wonderful things. Only I wish we loved Him more for loving us so much as He does."

"He loves you, I've no doubt, but"——

"But what, Willie? You don't mean that you think He does not love you?"

The boy looked up with a grim smile. "Likely He loves *me!* It looks like it, doesn't it?" And he looked down at his poor limbs.

"O Willie, poor boy, do you think He does not love you because He lets you be lame? I don't know, but it seems to me that He must love you all the more."

Again the grim smile, and a scornful sound between a laugh and a grunt.

"Oh, how I wish I could explain it!" said Bruey, getting very earnest. "If I were grown up, I could put it into words as the clergymen do, and then you would understand. Only I am quite sure about it in my mind; and, indeed, it isn't because He does not love you, but because He loves you very particularly." She hesitated for a moment. "Oh, I have just thought of something which will show you what I mean—you reminded me of it. That blind man, you know, he had been blind all his life, and a beggar too, so that must have been very bad and miserable indeed. And the Pharisees had good eyes, and were quite well off. But Jesus certainly loved the blind man best by a great deal, for, when the Pharisees had cast him out, He came and spoke to him all by himself, and told him He was the Son of God, and was so kind to him, that it showed He must have loved him very much. And I think the man must have been ever so glad that he had been blind, else Jesus would not have had so much to do with him. And, perhaps, if he had been able to see, he would never have seen Jesus at all, nor believed on Him."

"Where's that?"

"The story, do you mean? It is somewhere in St. John, but I can't recollect which chapter. I will find it when I go home."

"It's of no consequence," said Willie.

Mrs. Murray stepped out from Mrs. Fosbery's. Bruey heard the latter say, "Well, ma'am, I'll do as you say, and I hope she will have no more of this nonsense."

"O Mamma, is that where Hetty lives? I forgot to ask Willie about her, but I should like to see her."

"Hetty is gone out on an errand, but you shall come in with me to Mrs. Fayling's, and see her old mother-in-law, Bella's Grannie."

"Good morning, Willie."

"Good morning, ma'am, and miss."

Old Mrs. Fayling was in her arm-chair, and Bella was shyly standing on one foot, with her finger in her mouth, hanging on to the arm. Bruey spoke to her, but soon came and sat down by her mamma. Bella was not easy to talk to at any time, and Bruey could not bear being overheard by any grown-up people, even her mother.

Mrs. Murray read a little to the old woman, who leant forward to listen with great delight, lifting her hand and slowly moving her head at almost every verse, by way of expressing how good it was.

"Now my poor eyes is nigh gone, and I can't do nothing, it's all my comfort, a bit of reading. When Monday morning comes, I thinks, there's my kind lady a-coming again, and she'll read me the book. I don't get much hold of it, my memory's that bad, but it seems to serve me like for the day, and then I waits till next week. I'm a poor ignorant creature, but I do love them blessed words."

"Have you no one else to read to you?" asked Mrs. Murray.

"Emma had used to read, but she goes to work now. And I think my time will come 'fore Bella here can read. But her says the texts from school quite pretty, and that's a comfort."

"Bella's little teacher has come to see you, Mrs. Fayling: she will be glad to hear that she says her texts to you."

"Oh dear, miss, I *am* a poor creature, and I didn't know you. Well, sure, it is kind of you; I am afraid she gives you a sight of trouble, she's that heedless. Bella, my dear, did you make your curtsy to Miss Murray?"

"Oh, yes, Mrs. Fayling, she did. I think she tries to learn her texts better."

"It's a'most as good as the bit of reading, that's all my comfort to hear; it brings it all to my poor mind. I hope you'll please to bear with her, miss, for the texts is a comfort to her poor Grannie. Her says them over every day."

They did not stay long. "I have one more house to go to," said Mrs. Murray; "will you come in with me, or would you rather go and talk to Willie again?"

"I will come with you to the door, and then go back to Willie. O Mamma, I wish I might go and read to poor Mrs. Fayling."

"I do not see how that can be done, Bruey; I should not like you to come here alone."

Willie was deep in his magazine when Bruey came back to him.

"I've read six pages, and that is a quarter of the book," he said. "Books never seem to hold out long."

"Perhaps mamma will let me come again next week, and then I will bring you another. But suppose you could not see to read!"

"Quite too dreadful to suppose; things are bad enough without that."

"The time would be very long then, if you could neither read nor walk about. Would you not like some one to come and read to you then?"

"It is not likely I shall be blind, but no one would come if I were."

"But you would be glad if they did. And, O Willie, I know some one who can't walk and can't see, and who sits all the week wanting some one to come and read to her. And I should like to do it, but I must not. Oh, if you would, Willie?"

He fixed his great eyes on her, cross and curious both. "Who?"

"I'm sure you wouldn't mind, and I'm sure she would be *so* glad. It's old Mrs. Fayling; she says a bit of reading is all her comfort."

Mrs. Fayling! So that was all the young lady was driving at! What difference did it make to him that she wanted to be read to? She wasn't *his* Grannie. It was only those half-clergyman sort of people, scripture-readers, or some such name, that did that kind of thing.

Bruey's proposal was not very graciously met, but she did not soon give up when bent upon a thing, so she pleaded and persuaded till Willie said, "If I knew for certain that she would like *me* to read to her, and if I knew what to read to her, and got a nice book on purpose, why, perhaps I might."

"Wait a minute, Willie!" And she darted away, coming back in a minute or two quite triumphantly. "There! I have gone and asked her my own self, and she is as pleased—you can't think! And, Willie, I can tell you for certain what she would like. If you could find her that chapter about the blind man, I know she would think that beautiful, and I know there are some more very beautiful chapters just about there. Now, would you not promise me you would go in there a bit this afternoon and read it to her?"

Willie seemed to think it beneath his dignity to consent too easily.

Mrs. Murray was coming down the yard, and there was no time for more. But it did not seem hopeless, so Bruey trotted home with her mamma in good spirits.

"O Mamma, I felt so disappointed for a minute when you said I could not go and read to old Mrs. Fayling, and now I am so glad!"

"What now?"

"I do think I have almost persuaded that poor cripple boy to go and read to her; and that will be better, because he could read to her every day. What a strange boy he is, Mamma, he talks so gravely, and he does not use bad grammar, like some of the children do."

Mrs. Murray smiled. "I do think the Sunday-school has helped you in one thing, Bruey; you never would see the difference between nominative and objective before, but you seem to have got hold of it now that you hear the children say, 'Her said,' and 'I gives it to she.' And certainly no instances of 'A verb must agree with its nominative case in number and person,' impressed it upon you so much as hearing that 'they goes to church,' or that 'we isn't a coming.' But as for Willie, I suppose his very nice way of speaking is partly because he reads so much, and partly because he had an uncle, who was a rather superior man. He had been a gentleman's servant, but was ill at the Fosbery's house for a long time—years, I fancy, and it was he who taught Willie to read."

"Was he a good man, Mamma?"

"I never saw him, dear; he died before I had that district."

CHAPTER V.

PEPPERY.

BRUEY had hardly reached her room, when Percy knocked at her door. "Here, I want you to tie a bit of rag round my finger. I cut it a little while ago, and it won't stop bleeding. Don't look pitiful now, it's nothing; only tie it up, that's a good girl; no hurry, I've got my handkerchief tight round it. Hallo, Bruey! where did you get that?" And Percy made an angry dash at the yellow book which she had left on the drawers.

"I'm very sorry, Percy; I found it in your drawer. I did not know you would not like me to have it, as you always lend me your books."

"What business have you at my drawer?"

"Don't you remember? you told me yesterday that I might get your magazines out of it for Willie Fosbery."

"But I did not tell you to get this, did I? Hark you, Bruey, don't you go taking my books again without leave."

"Please don't be so angry, Percy; indeed I won't again. But why are you so vexed? Here is the rag, where is your finger?"

"Oh, it's all right," said he, changing his tone. "You wouldn't care for that book, I know, so it's no use your having it. There, take care, wrap it tight, so that it can't slip; it does not bleed so much now, I needn't have troubled you. I say, Bruey, don't you go and tell Aunt you took my book; she might not be pleased with you."

"Why not?"

"She would think you had no business to go ferreting in my drawers, and you did not mean to do it, so there's no occasion for you to go fussing about it. You mind what I say, now! Thank you, that will do first-rate."

Bruey was exceedingly mystified as to why she should not tell her mamma such a simple thing. But Percy did not stay for further explanation.

After dinner, Bruey went to a little hanging cupboard which filled a corner behind the outer door of her room. She took down sundry frocks and jackets, and hung them up again. Then she went to her drawers, and turned over everything, shaking out some things, and laying them back again, finding at last two or three articles, which she put on her table. "It would not be fair to ask to give away what I am wearing myself, or Mamma would only have to buy me new things instead. But something might be managed with these."

She carried her selection down to her mamma. "Are you very busy, Mamma; could you look here?"

"What's all this, Bruey?"

"You remember I told you about Mary Shelton tearing her frock, and I am sure they are very poor, and I should so like to give her one."

"But you have not one that I can let you spare yet, and it would be too large if you had."

"Yes, I know; but please look here. Here is this purple petticoat; I can't possibly wear it any more, it is so much too short for me now, and it can't be let down. I thought this would do for a frock-skirt for her quite well, if I turned it up a little round the bottom, and you would show me how. And then, Mamma, there is the cape like my grey alpaca; you said you were sorry I had it made, because it does not suit me, and you like my silk jacket better with that frock,— would not this about make a body for her?"

Mrs. Murray turned it over. "It might; but the sleeves would have to be very tight."

"But it *would* make it, would it not? If you would cut it out, and put it ready for me, I could do it in the evenings while Percy is at his lessons. And then, Mamma, look, this cloth jacket is so tight I can hardly get it on at all; might I not give her this?"

"My dear, it would look like a greatcoat on that little thing, if she is no taller than Hetty Fosbery, as I understood you."

"Oh, but I could make it smaller, could I not? that is, if you would show me."

"Don't you see what a pity it would be to spoil a nice jacket like this by altering it to fit such a very little child? It would be waste to do that."

Bruey looked vexed. She did not like to be checked in any of her little plans; and surely it was much nicer to give away things without calculating. She thought it would be rather fine to give Mary a whole outfit at once, with some work of her own in each part of it.

"I should so *like* to give it her," she said, not very amiably.

"I want you to have a little sense and patience. There is very seldom any-thing lost by waiting. If you put this jacket by for a little while, we shall be sure to find someone who will be very glad of it, without needing to cut it down and spoil it. A poor mother is always more glad of a garment for an older girl, be-cause it costs her less to manage something for the very little ones."

Bruey quite saw the sense of it, but still did not like it, and said so.

"There is such a thing as showing temper and selfishness while professing to wish to do good," said her mother.

Now she felt very naughty. She did not mean to be selfish; was it likely, when she even planned to do the sewing as well as give away her things? And it was too bad to talk about "temper"; she knew she had not *felt* good-tempered, but what had she said? Only that she would *like* to do what she wished. And who wouldn't? If Mamma would not say things like that, it would be much easier to be good. Miss Allison didn't, and Uncle Henry didn't, and she could be good with them, she was sure. So she pouted and scowled, while her moth-er folded up the jacket.

"I can't possibly set the work for you this afternoon, so you had better take the things upstairs till I can see to it. What would Willie Fosbery think of you if he saw your face now? and all about nothing!"

Bruey went off with the things, and Mrs. Murray sat down to write a letter. But she only dated it, and then sat with her pen in her hand, thinking. "She is wonderfully improved. How trying she used to be, poor little thing! But I see she tries to do better, and control her temper; and why should I wonder that she fails? Do not I fail too? Ah, Lord, Thou knowest! Poor little thing! what conflicts she will have to go through with sin and self! She does not know much about it yet. It is so easy to *do* good, and so hard to *be* good. Am I too hard upon her? But if I did not speak so to her, I am afraid it would be all sur-face-work. Poor little fatherless one! no one will show her her faults when I am gone. I feel sure the grace of God is at work: but oh, the years it takes to learn one's sinfulness and helplessness! O Father, guide me, and help me to help my child, *Thy* child."

What was Bruey doing? There had been a great struggle with pride and temper, and she felt as if there were two Brueys inside her, disputing together. *No. I.* said, "I'm sure I could be good if Mamma did not say such things; that is just what makes me naughty." *No. II.* said, "That does not quite account for it; because if I were not naughty inside, I should not be so easily provoked; I should be patient, and answer quite sweetly." *No. I.*—"But I am sure all I want-ed was to be good and kind to Mary." *No. II.*—"But I wonder why I did not want to do the *most* good, as Mamma explained to me?" *No. I.*—"It wasn't likely I should care to give things to folks I don't know. Mary is in my own class." *No. II.*—"Then I only wanted to give it because she is in my class; so it was selfish, and Mamma was quite right." *No. I.*—"But she needn't have said so. She might let me alone. I don't like being made out to be wrong." *No. II.*—"Then I was even worse than she said, for there was pride as well as temper and selfishness." *No. I.*—"At all events, I was not very bad this time; I did not say cross things which I could have said." *No. II.*—"But, oh dear! I wish I had not spoken crossly at all." *No. I.*—"It's no use trying." *No. II.*—"Only two hours ago I was talking to Willie Fosbery. What would he think! Mamma was right there. About Jesus, too—Jesus my Saviour. I will kneel down and tell Him all about it, and ask Him to forgive me and help me." *No. I.*—"There is Mamma coming upstairs, I will wait till she is gone; I should not like her to come in suddenly, and find me kneeling down." *No. II.*—"If I wait, I know I shall not do it, and then I shall feel unhappy all day. Besides, it is not Mamma after all, only Jane's step." *No. I.*—"I really ought to go and practise at once; it is past the time, and Mamma will be vexed again." *No. II.*—"No, I *must* pray first."

So the better Bruey prevailed this time; that is, not Bruey's own resolution, but the new nature which God had given her, and against which the old nature—the *naughty* Bruey—fought so hard. The greatest difficulty seemed to be that she was always being taken unawares; temptations hardly ever came when and where she was on the look-out, but quite unexpectedly and suddenly. She found it out afresh this afternoon. How could she see pride and selfishness and temper waylaying her when she went down only to plan a Sunday dress for poor little Mary? So she told this difficulty to the never-weary Ear; she felt so very helpless about it, that there seemed no chance for her *but* to do so, and to ask to be kept from sin, as she could not keep herself.

She practised famously that afternoon, and got the lessons prepared in very good time.

She went out in the garden. It was a glorious evening, and the fine weather of the past few days had brought the buds out on the lilacs, and given quite a tinge of faint green to the sunny side of the hedges. After a while, Percy appeared. "I am so glad you are home in good time to-day, Percy, it is such a splendid afternoon. Wouldn't you come with me to the primrose wood?"

"There won't be time," said he. "Aunt is so punctual."

Bruey ran into the house. "Mamma, we have a favour to ask. Would you mind having tea half an hour later? then Percy and I would just have time to go to the primrose wood. He does not care to go on a half-holiday, but he would come to-day. The primroses are all out now, not just a few little short-stalked things. Do, Mamma, if you don't mind."

"Very well."

There was something in the tone which touched Bruey. She put her arm round her mother's neck and kissed her, whispering, "I will try, Mamma. And I was *so* sorry."

She was glad when she had said this, although her mamma seemed to take very little notice of it.

They had a good half-hour among the primroses; and these were so plentiful that they gathered a basketful, and then filled Percy's pocket-handkerchief.

"What do you want with such a lot?" asked Percy, stopping to watch Bruey, who was gathering as if her life depended on it.

"That I can't tell you! Only, when there are such quantities, and no one to miss them, one seems as if one must go on gathering as many as ever one can. You like gathering them too, don't you?"

"Yes; but I don't know why. They are no use, they only die."

"Mamma likes to have them in the vases, so that is something."

"But we have got twice as many as you could cram into the vases."

"Well, never mind that. I can put them in a soup plate with some moss. It is such fun gathering them."

"We must come home now, though, Bruey, else we shall be benighted and have the crier sent after us."

"I suppose we must; but I wish we need not go yet."

"You might feel for me, then; I am glad you don't always like over-punctuality."

Bruey took this as meant for a little hit at her mother, who was so often annoyed by Percy's lateness in the morning, and had once been still more so by a note from his master, requesting that she would see that he came to school in better time. Nothing made Bruey feel more angry than the least thing of this kind. Percy had no intention of either vexing Bruey, or of hitting at his aunt. He was thinking of his master, and went on—"It is such a horrid nuisance to be tied to punctual folks. And the more punctual they are, the more certain their clocks are to go different from other people's."

Bruey gathered up her primroses, and commenced stalking homewards magnificently. "Our clocks always go by railway time," she said, holding her head up very straight.

"That's what they always say; and if it was railway time three weeks ago, they cram it down your throat as if they'd proved it out of Euclid. I do believe punctuality is a sort of pride; with some folks it is."

"You had better not go on that way!" said Bruey, defiantly.

"What way? What on earth do you mean? Whatever is the matter?"

He might well ask, for she was marching along like a general, and looking as stiff and fierce as possible. Not a syllable.

"Really, Bruey, you are too much for a fellow. What has one said?"

"You know quite well, and you had better not go on."

Percy was puzzled, and whistled—his usual resource.

Presently he tried again, in quite a troubled tone—"I say, Bruey, I *really* don't know what you mean! Don't start off this way. At any rate, let one know what's the matter."

"I think it *is* matter when you go and say things like that at Mamma. She is very kind to you, and it isn't her fault that you have impositions when you are late. You would have had plenty more if it hadn't been for her punctuality."

The state of the case dawned upon him. "My dear cousin, I was not thinking about Aunt, and I could not imagine what made you get up in the boughs in that style."

"Yes, you were; you said nasty things about punctual people being proud. And Mamma is punctual, and you meant her, and I don't like it."

"If you can't believe I am speaking the truth when I am, I suppose it doesn't matter whether I do or not. I tell you I never said a word about Aunt, and I wasn't thinking about her either."

She strutted on. It is more easy to get up in the boughs than to get down again. But she was not very comfortable; it was not likely Percy would tell a story; and if he had not meant her mamma at all, what a pity to have made such an unchristian fuss for nothing!

As she did not speak, Percy went on—"One must mind what one says; I did not know you were so touchy."

"I am *not* touchy; I am only touchy about Mamma," she said, heartily wishing she could get out of the little scrape with due dignity—"that is all the difference."

"Then you might be nice and pleasant now, when you know I did not mean her." Percy had a great mind to suggest that she was too proud to be "nice" all at once on finding her mistake; but he thought this would make further mischief, and was sufficiently amiable and sensible to refrain. "If you would put a jacket on some morning, and come with me, and see Mr. Harston pull out his turnip and declare it is railway time, and set impositions accordingly, when I'm positive half the clocks in Rilverton have not begun to think of striking, you would understand what I said."

"But if he was unpunctual at one end, he would be so at the other too, and you would not like to be kept at work after *your* watch said it was twelve o'clock. I like the other way much best. If I know when I begin, I know when I have done, and that is Mamma's way."

"Yes, I daresay it is best, and all that; but it's no good having your boots a beautiful fit if you have a great corn. I quite believe in the beauty and excellence of punctuality, but it is a bore sometimes. Cold mornings, now; how horrid it is to hear the bell ring to the minute then! Mind, Bruey dear, I really don't mean that I think Aunt is wrong to have the bell rung to the minute," he added, soothingly.

Bruey was quite down out of the boughs now, and felt humbled by Percy's good humour. She had wished for some time that she could venture to coax him really to try to come down in time for prayers every morning, but she could not possibly say anything of that sort now that she had been so fiery and cross. And she had been wishing, too, that she might even venture to say something more to him. She was pretty sure that if he said any prayers at all in the morning, they must be very short ones, because he certainly was not always even out of bed when the bell rang; and sometimes when she had felt as if her own little prayers had really helped and strengthened her, and made her feel glad and bright, she did *so* wish Percy felt just the same, only a great deal better. Which would surely be the case, she thought, because he was so much better than she was to begin with. But what could she say *now!*

Further, there was a curious fancy in her mind, which she had not put into shape, which made her say, "That reminds me—did you hear a noise last night?"

"A noise? I don't think I woke from the time I went to sleep till Jane called me. Do you see that robin, Bruey? there, hopping on the top of that hedge?"

"Yes, I see. Why, I wonder we did not wake you. Mamma went downstairs after eleven o'clock, and I got out of bed and listened, and I thought I saw a light under your door. I was so frightened. Percy, *didn't* you hear us?"

"Well, let me see; now you say, I think I did hear something. But folks can fancy anything if they lie awake and listen. We should have heard more of it if it had been anything."

"What was it like, what you heard?"

"Oh, I don't know. You'll get nervous to-night if you think about noises and lights. Hallo! there's a violet on the other side of the ditch. I'll get it."

It was odd that Percy was not more curious about the disturbance. But he evidently did not care about the information, so the violet was picked, and a few more found, and in a few minutes more they reached Calton Terrace, and heard Rilverton clocks striking half-past six, and the tea-bell ringing just as they got in. Percy had guessed the time well.

CHAPTER VI.

PRIMROSE CANDLESTICKS.

WEDNESDAY morning was dark and windy, after the still and brilliant evening before. It had rained, and meant to rain again. The clouds drove across the sky in an angry, determined way, as if they had made up their minds once for all that if the young buds thought it was Spring, and insisted on coming out, they should have as uncomfortable a time of it as possible. The buds looked grey and dismal, instead of shining out in " emerald and gold," as they did in Tuesday evening's sunlight, and the branches shivered and creaked.

But the buds did not know that the clouds were very kind friends after all, and would do them a great deal of good, and make them much more beautiful by the time the next fine weather came.

Bruey had just begun her music when Jane came in.

"Miss Bruey, there's a little girl wants to see you."

She jumped up. "Who is it, Jane?"

"I did not ask her name, miss; but she's a poor-looking, peakèd little thing" ("peakèd" signifying thin in the face).

She went to the kitchen, and there was Sophy Willis, looking very small and miserable, and holding the hand of Jim Willis, who was smaller and more miserable still. Sophy brightened up on seeing her teacher, and produced a bottle for more cough mixture, giving a pull to Jim, who was cowering behind her, to bring him into position. Bruey spoke kindly to both of them, and let them sit down near the fire, while she went to her mamma for the medicine.

"They do look so starved and wretched, Mamma, I wish you would give them something—some money, I mean."

"That would not do much good, I expect, if they are the sort of people I fancy. I will come down presently and see. They can wait a few minutes."

Bruey went back to them.

"Well, Sophy, tell me how they all are? Is baby better?"

"Yes, teacher; but she coughs, nights, and so does Jim and Matty, and that makes them cross, days."

"And don't you get cross too?" asked Bruey kindly, as she looked at the little old face, so much younger in years, but older in cares than her own, and wondered for a minute how cross she would feel if she were in Sophy's place!

Sophy gave a little laugh, and said, "If I was to be cross, I should have to be cross all day! It's not so bad to do with them when it's fine, but they make me cross sometimes when it rains."

"Why when it rains, Sophy?"

"'Cause they can't get out, teacher, and gets tired of being in the house, and gets in mother's way, and then they gets cross, and then they make the baby cry, and then mother's cross."

"Can't they play with anything?"

"They haven't got anything to play with, without they've got some stones off the path. The little Checkettses next door have got a doll, and puts her to bed, but Jim and Matty haven't nothing." Sophy was only seven years old; but to hear her talk, you would have thought playthings were only meant for much smaller children than herself—the little woman who had to take care of others instead of being cared for herself. She looked towards the window with a mournfully weather-wise shake of the head. "It will rain all day, I know, when it begins!" And the home prospects for the day were dismal indeed, to judge by her face.

"I know something I can give you for them to play with to-day!" cried Bruey, delightedly. She ran off, leaving Sophy in the act of giving another pull of adjustment to her brother, and saying, "Now, if you sit good, the lady will bring you something to play with."

She came back with two great soup-plates full of primroses, which she set on the table. "There! should you like to have those?" Sophy looked as if she would like them very much indeed, but Jim looked sour and disappointed. He wanted something to play with, not flowers to look at, and too pretty to pull about. But Bruey took them out of the water, and put them all in a heap into a paper bag.

"See now, Sophy and Jim, you can take these home and play with them all the morning. Look, I will show you how to make chains of them; see, split the stalk, and put another primrose through it, now split that and put another through!" and she held up a chain of four or five primroses before Jim's eyes. "Jim could do it as well as you, Sophy, and would not Matty be pleased to watch you? You could make yards and yards with these. And look, Jim, Sophy can put the primroses on the floor in classes; there are seven little ones for the children, and a big one for the teacher. Look at them, sitting all in a row, Jim!"

Jim began to smile, and slipped off the chair to get close to them.

"Oh, there's a naughty primrose," continued Bruey, "come to school with a dirty face; we will send that one home again to the bag; and now, Jim, see if you can pick out a good little primrose with a nice clean face to send to school instead." She laughed at her own device, and Sophy had visions of playing at school with the flowers, and keeping Jim and Matty contented thereby all through a rainy afternoon. "Now we'll make some rings!" said Bruey; and she stuck the stalks of two or three into the middle of the flower, looping them into a little chain of rings. "And now we'll make some candlesticks!"—which was the most delightful suggestion of all, though it only consisted in pulling off the flower of the primrose and setting it upside down on the table, with a tiny bit of stalk stuck into the small tube to represent a candle.

Mrs. Murray came in with the bottle, and while she was hearing from Sophy that she "had used to go to the infant school last summer, for a bit, till baby came," and that "Jim would have gone this winter, on'y his cough was so bad Mother wouldn't send him," Bruey slipped away to the pantry to reconnoitre, and came back to whisper to her mamma that the breakfast things were just brought out, and there was some tea left in the pot quite warm, and some toast not finished, and might she give it to the little Willises? She had leave, and putting a little more hot water from the urn, soon had quite a nice cup of tea for the children. They drank the tea and ate the toast so hungrily, that it was plain they had not had too much breakfast beforehand.

Meanwhile, Mrs. Murray had noticed Jim's cough, and also the fact that his small feet were worse off than if he had come barefoot, having an old pair of shoes with a slit in each, just enough to let the wet soak in and make his feet cold and damp the first time he trod in a puddle. And small boys always do tread in puddles if there are puddles to tread in, so no wonder Jim's cough had resisted the virtue of the cough mixture. So she went and wrote a note, and gave it to Sophy, telling her to take it, on her way home with Jim, to a certain shoemaker to whom it was addressed, and to wait till he had read it.

When they went away, looking much less miserable than when they came, Bruey went back to her music, and got through that and her lessons without any misfortunes. When she had finished, it was raining heavily, and there could be no going out.

"Now," said Mrs. Murray, "I could see about the things you wanted to give that other child." Bruey went to fetch them down, and her mamma called out, as she left the room, "You can bring down that hat of yours, if you like."

She brought the petticoat and cape, and the Sunday hat, wondering what was going to be done as to that.

"You have not brought the cloth jacket," said Mrs. Murray; "I want to look at that again."

She fetched it, and laid it on the table, where her mother had spread out the alpaca cape, and was contriving to get a body out of it.

"Hand me that piece of lining, Bruey; and then, if you like, you can unpick the trimming of your hat while I get this ready for you."

Her mother did not seem inclined to enter into any conversation on the latter subject, so Bruey made no remark, but set to work, very much pleased, and wondering considerably what had brought this about. Not that she was very much surprised, for Mrs. Murray often objected to things at first to which she afterwards consented. She saw the corner of a piece of velvet peeping out of a work-basket, but she asked no questions, and the hat was untrimmed and the body cut out in silence.

"Mamma, I have done this; can you give me anything else to do?"

"You might tack this lining and stuff together if you think you can keep it straight and flat." When the body was cut out, Mrs. Murray took up the jacket. "Try it on, Bruey, and let me see." She did so. "There, I think it will do exactly."

"What for, Mamma?"

"For Alice Fosbery. Her mother tells me she has had some trouble with her lately, and also cannot afford to keep her at school any longer, and is going to try to get her a little place. But a girl can't go untidy, especially if she gets a little nursemaid's place, and this jacket would be just what she most wants."

"Will it not be too small? She is nearly fourteen, and quite as tall as I am."

"But she is very slight; not half the width across the shoulders that you are; and as the jacket is plenty long enough, and only too tight for you, I expect it will fit her beautifully. It does not want anything done to it. If you are a good girl you shall take it down yourself, if I go, next Monday or Tuesday." Mrs. Murray folded it up, and turned to the purple petticoat. "This will not take long," she said; "I will pin it for you, and begin it, and then you can go on with it quite well."

They went on till Percy came past the window, and Bruey ran to the door to meet him, and then the table had to be cleared that the cloth might be laid for dinner. She was going to carry all upstairs. "Leave that hat," said Mrs. Murray. She obeyed, and went off with the rest of her work.

CHAPTER VII.

ONE USE OF A CUSHION.

NEXT Sunday morning the Faylings and Fosberys were at school before Bruey.

"There's Miss Murray," said Emma.

"She's got another new hat," said Alice. "No, it isn't; I believe it's the very same done up different, and no roses. They were all as good as new, I could see. Well, I shouldn't have done that if I had been Miss Murray."

"What have you done with yours, Alice?"

"Why, don't you know? The flowers are not fastened, only pinned, and so I take them out to come to Sunday school, and stick them in when I go at night with Lizzie Telf and sit in the gallery at St. John's. But, only think, Mother's made up her mind to let me leave school and go for a place, and I shan't be always pinning and unpinning then; I shall wear what I like."

"But shall you not come to school if they will let you? I should not like to give up school this long time yet."

"I shall see," replied Alice, grandly; "it will depend on circumstances."

"You have not got a place yet," said Clara Jones.

"And you will wish yourself back at day-school when you have," said Emma; "I know *I* do."

"Other folks may get better places," retorted Alice. "I wouldn't go out to work for anything; I mean to get a nurse place, and go out with a perambulator." Thereupon Miss Anstey came in, and Alice had to keep the rest of her intentions to herself.

"Ah, Hetty," said Bruey, when she had received the regulation curtsies and "Good morning, teacher," "I was at Gilling's Yard last week, and you were not at home. I was so sorry."

For the first time in her school history, Bella spoke of her own accord. "*I* was," she said, with a sort of grin, which would have been a smile if produced by any other child. But Bella did not deal in smiles; indeed, her finger was too much in her mouth for any such article to be very common.

"Please, teacher, won't you come again? I won't be out next time, not unless I must," said Hetty. "Our Willie wants you."

"How is Willie?"

"Please, teacher, he's been pretty cheerful. And I fetched him lots of things, teacher!"

Bruey wondered what this meant for an instant, but recollected her counsel to Hetty the Sunday before. Before she could decide how to answer this self-satisfied little speech, Hetty went on. "Please, teacher, Mary Shelton wishes you would come and see her." And little Mary seconded the small spokeswoman with very pleading eyes.

"I cannot promise that, Mary; but you may come up to me on, let me see, Tuesday morning. Come before you go to school."

"Please, teacher, may I come and show her the way? I know where it is," said Hetty.

"No, Hetty, she will find it quite easily. But I hope I shall come and see Willie to-morrow, and then I will tell you if you may come up some morning. You shall all come in turn," she added, seeing Betsy Barnett, one of her new girls, look as if she would very much like to come too.

Sophy Willis came in, quite bright.

"Well, Sophy?"

"They was *so* good, teacher! All day!"

Poor little Sophy! It was something to have made one long, dismal, rainy day pleasant and easy for that weary little old woman of seven years old. And how nice it was to look forward to Tuesday morning, by which time Mary's frock would be finished. The poor old torn barège need not appear next Sunday.

As the classes filed out for church under Miss Allison's review, Bruey fancied her smile, as "Eighth Class" passed, was particularly personal and affectionate to herself, and wondered why. She forgot about her hat.

It rained in the afternoon, so Bruey had to hurry home without waiting for the leisurely walk up with Miss Allison, which she hoped would come to pass some Sunday.

After tea it was worse still, and Mrs. Murray having decided that it would be too wet to go down to church, left the room.

"Come and be nice, Bru!" said Percy, lolling on the sofa.

"Being nice means different things; what does it mean now?"

"Come and amuse me, that's being nice; I'm as moped as an old cat. Don't go off, now."

Bruey stood and hesitated. If she stayed with Percy, she would very likely miss her little Sunday evening prayer and reading altogether; and if she did that, she would be sure to get wrong in some way. But then if she left him it would make Sunday evening duller still to him, and he did not seem inclined to read or do anything but kick on the sofa. She said to herself, "What shall I do?" and yet it was hardly saying it to herself, for it was as if her heart looked up while she said it, and she wished God would make her do the right thing. So it was a prayer, though she did not call it such.

"Percy, I will come down to you in five minutes."

"All square; mind you do."

And she went. She would make the most of the five minutes, she thought, so she went straight to her seat under the window, and took her Bible. But she could not quite make up her mind what to read, and turned over the leaves. What did she read last Sunday evening? Something she meant to go on with, she knew, but she could not recollect where it was. Then she thought she would look for and read part of what Willie Fosbery was to read to old Mrs. Fayling. She found it at last, but read only four verses. For she stopped to think about the fourth—"*I must work the works of Him that sent Me while it is day; the night cometh, when no man can work.*" "I wonder if I shall have a long time to work. And I wonder if I am doing all the work I ought. There does not seem much to do, only little things. I will pray about this now." She knelt down, and asked that God would show her if there was any other work for her to do, and give it her, as He had given her the Sunday-school class. And then that He would help her to do all the little things right which she did find to do. And then she remembered that it was her day to pray for Percy, though since she had put his initials on her card, she had prayed for him every day as well as for her little girls. So she prayed for him, and while she prayed she wished more than ever that he might be a safe and happy Christian boy; and as she wished, she began to wonder whether *this* was work laid before her to do; and then her eye fell again on the verse still open before her, and she prayed that God would help her to help Percy even that very day. For what if the night should come, what if he should be ill, and the doctors not let her speak to him! Rap-a-rap, rap! came at the door, and Bruey started up. "Come in!" she said.

"How do you do, Miss Punctual? Some time since I had the pleasure of seeing you! This isn't being nice, Bruey; you were coming back in five minutes, and I have kicked the sofa cushion for eight minutes and a half, and it will be the worse for wear if you don't come soon."

He closed the door and came forward. Bruey seated him on her box, and sat down on the floor beside him.

"I don't think you ever sat on my box before. Isn't it a comfortable corner? Only you can't kick there, else *I* should be the worse for wear. I was coming down directly; wait till I have a watch like you, and then see how punctual I would be!"

"You are not badly off here; I like this," said Percy, settling his back comfortably into the corner. "I would have a cushion, if I were you, though."

Bruey jumped up, and fetched her own pillow from the next room, gravely presenting it: "There, Mr. Sultan, allow me to put this behind your royal back."

Did anybody ever know a boy that had not a weakness for being made comfortable? or a boy that would not be waited on hand and foot, if he only had the chance? It is quite enough to prove our descent from Orientals. So Percy, being a boy, naturally accepted the pillow, and let Bruey make him very comfortable therewith. It was not a bad idea, nor any waste of time; for another observable peculiarity of boys in general is, that they are much more inclined to be "good" when they are comfortable. Suppose you want to keep three of them quiet and attentive for a whole half-hour or more on a Sunday afternoon, while you talk to them or question them, nothing answers better than to take the smallest on your lap, and get him to nestle down as luxuriously as possible, and settle the two others with a cushion apiece at opposite ends of the sofa. They will be so astonishingly good! The effect might wear off, so it is only recommended on emergencies.

"There, that is first-rate. Is this where you always come on Sunday evenings when you go off and leave me to the dulls?"

"Yes, I like that corner for several reasons. I could tell you one. No, I won't though!"

"Come now, what's the mystery? I'll undertake to tell you six, if you'll tell me the one you were going to for the seventh."

For Bruey's change of look, and of colour too, roused Percy's curiosity, as the words themselves would not have done. A sweet memory of that little corner had flashed up in her mind, and with it the thought that, if she only could possibly summon up courage to tell Percy about it, it might make him more inclined to think and seek than any such "talking to" as she was likely to accomplish. But could she venture? She never had told any one anything that passed in that sacred little corner. Still, the impression came strongly upon her that it was perhaps the best opportunity she could have, and this the best way to use it. She hesitated and smiled, and then said, "I'll see; perhaps I can't put it into words. O Percy, I almost wish I had not said that."

Of course Percy was determined to have it now.

"All right, you did say it, and I'm going to hear it. Perhaps it will turn out to be one of my six. First, then, you like this corner because it is so comfortable. And, secondly, because it is not meant to be a seat at all, and so you like it out of contrariety."

Bruey smiled and nodded, and said, "Go on."

"Thirdly—thirdly—oh, I know! because you can see the bell-turret of your dearly-beloved school. And fourthly, because I have no business to come and bother you here."

"O Percy! you know it does not bother me."

"How should I know anything of the sort, when you make a point of cutting me just when I want you? Fifthly, because you can put your elbows on the table, and you mustn't do that downstairs. Sixthly—well, let me see; are you sure the last wasn't sixthly? Because —because"——

"I will help you now, Percy, and tell you a real one. Sixthly, then, because I like to see the sunsets here over the elms and the towers and the hills. It feels so quiet, somehow, and makes it easier to—to—to think about what one wants to think about."

"Isn't it always easy to think about what one wants to think about? I find it pretty hard to do exactly the other thing, to think about what one does *not* want to think about,—one's lines and verbs and all that."

"Percy," said Bruey, with a desperate resolve that she would say out what was in her heart, even if it made it beat very much, "I think you know what I mean. I meant, easier to think about the things one *ought* to think about—you know what—good things, heavenly things. O Percy! I do want to think about them more, and I daresay, down in the bottom of your heart, you do too. Only I fancy it must be a little harder for boys than for girls." She stooped, and leaned her arm on Percy's knee as she sat on the floor below him, and looked up at the cloudy sky. He was sobered, again much more by the reality and earnestness of her manner than by anything she said. It *was* harder for boys than for girls, he was satisfied, but even Bruey did not seem to find it always easy, and that was a kind of consolation by contraries. He looked at her for a moment, and said—

"Was your particular reason something to do with this sort of thing?"

The question was a great help.

"Yes. It was last autumn, when the days were shortening in, so that there was twilight directly after tea, and I had been very unhappy, because—O Percy! I daresay you know what it feels like!—because I was afraid I should never go to heaven, and so afraid of God. And I came up one evening after tea and sat down here, and opened my Bible; I had never done so before, except morning and evening when Mamma told me to read a chapter; and I did not know where to

look, but I wondered if I should find anything to comfort me if I went on looking. I could not see anything but histories of wars, and strings of queer names,
at first; and then I turned over Exodus, and that seemed to be all about curtains
and cubits; and then, all at once, I saw the words, '*There I will meet with thee.*' I
could not tell why, but they sounded beautiful and kind, and as if one need not
be afraid to meet Him '*there*' if one only knew where '*there*' was. So I looked to
see. I could not understand it very well, but it was something about the 'mercy-
seat'; and I remembered a hymn about it, that Mamma had set me to learn,
and it seemed to have something to do with prayer. So I thought perhaps '*there*'
meant '*here*,' this very corner; and I knelt down and prayed, and asked God to
make it come true, and to let me come near to Him and love Him, and not feel
so miserable and frightened. I did not know exactly what to pray, but the words
came back to me over and over again, and it seemed like a real promise."

"I like your telling me all this, Bruey," said Percy, very gravely. "But did it
ever come quite true?"

"Well, I don't know, but it was something like it. After that the words used
to keep coming to me, and they seemed to make me want to come and kneel
down here, and I came every evening in the twilight. But I felt so naughty, and
the more I tried to be good the naughtier I felt; and then I thought if even dear
Mamma was so often vexed with me, what must God think, when He could see
all the naughty thoughts and feelings that she did not know of at all. O Percy! I
do not know how to go on telling you!" And she bent her hot little face down
upon the hand which rested on Percy's knee. He put his hand very gently, and
almost reverently, upon her hair, stroking it slowly.

"Go on, dear," he said, in a very low voice, "do tell me the rest; I always
wondered what people felt like, when——: go on, Bruey darling."

So she had to go on. "Then one evening it was worse than ever, for I
thought, there is that beautiful promise, and God cannot keep it, because I am
so wicked; I come here with all my sins, and more of them every day, and how
can He meet me with all these? And it seemed as if they were a great, dark,
high wall between Him and me, and as if it would only get darker and higher
every day I lived. I did not know what to do, for I could not pray any more, I
only cried all the time; and then I thought, Oh! if Jesus only knew, He would
surely be sorry for me, and help me. But then, all at once, I thought, Why, He
does know, He *must* know, and perhaps He is listening all the time, and waiting
for me to speak to Him! And then I told Him all about it; I felt quite sure He
was listening, and that my not being able to see Him did not make any difference, any more than it would if I were talking to you in the dark. I don't know
whether it was praying—it was just telling Him, and I could do that though I

had not felt able to pray, but perhaps it was all the same. And then "——— She stopped; could she tell even this? She never meant to tell any one, but she did want Percy to know how good and kind that dear Saviour had been to her. And perhaps no one else would ever tell him anything of the kind, or of course they would do it much better. "And then "———

"Then what, dear?"

Bruey suddenly raised her head, and Percy saw that her eyes were shining, with what hardly seemed tears, and yet they were wet. "Then, O Percy! I was so glad—while I was telling Him all about it, the words came into my mind, '*Thy sins be forgiven thee!*' I don't mean that I heard them, but it was almost the same thing; not as if I had thought of them myself, but as if they were sent quite fresh into my heart. And then I thought that it was His own answer to me because it was just what I wanted, and He must know; and then it did seem so good and kind of Him to send it into my mind and to make me so glad, that I had to begin again and tell Him so, and thank Him. It seemed as if God were not far off at all then, but quite near, and yet I was not afraid any more, because He was so kind, and I could not help loving Him instead."

Bruey was quite right in supposing that no one else had told Percy such things. To him it had always seemed a far-off and grown-up sort of business, and he was content that it should be so, because he did not like feeling uncomfortable, which he always did if he thought about religion. But here was his little cousin, younger than himself, yet having found what he had never set himself to seek. It must be very nice to feel as Bruey did; was there any chance of his ever being like that? He had heard two or three sermons which had frightened him a little, and made him wonder what would become of him if he were killed in a railway accident, or something over which he had no control; for he could not imagine dying of illness, never having had a doctor, except for chicken-pox. But this was a different thing; nothing to frighten him, but bringing a sense of tender longing to feel the same, and to be able to love Jesus; and a new feeling, that it was not a far-off or grown-up thing after all. They sat quite silent together for a little while, Percy pondering and wishing, Bruey wonderfully happy. For this confession had stirred up all the old love and gladness; and the two promises freshened up into all their first sweetness, as if the very quoting them to Percy were a renewing of them to herself.

Presently she said, "Now you know why I like my corner so much. I did not care about it before, but nearly everything seemed different after that."

"I think I shouldn't mind being you, Bruey," said Percy.

"I don't think it would be a good exchange for you in most things. But, Percy, do you mind my saying something? may I?"

"To be sure; I told you I liked to hear you talk."

"When I feel glad about what I have been telling you about, I do so wish you felt glad too. Perhaps you do, but"——

He answered the "but" plainly.

"No, Bruey, I'm bad enough, but I'm not a hypocrite; I *don't* feel glad like you mean, only glad for you, but"——

Another "but"! Though they had so far broken the ice, it was not all melted, and both were more or less shy.

She took his hand, and said—

"Percy dear, do ask Jesus to make you glad. He will, I know."

"I don't know; you are different."

"No, indeed! Except that I am not so nice as you. But it says, '*There is no difference.*' I don't know how it goes on, but it is something about calling on Him. Besides, it says, '*Thou art the same,*' and so He can't be different to you to what He is to me. O Percy, if you would only begin and ask Him!"

"*You* ask Him."

"So I do; I asked Him every day last week. But you must ask Him too—to-night and to-morrow morning. Won't you?"

"I daresay I shall to-night, but I shall be sleepy in the morning; and then I bundle on my clothes, and then it is time to come down, and past it too, generally."

Bruey considered. "But Jane calls you?"

"Yes, but I go to sleep again."

"Suppose I come across and give three good taps at your door directly after Jane has been, before you have had time to get too comfortable again. Would not that remind you, and wouldn't you try to get up, so as to have time to pray and read? You will be so glad afterwards, if you make up your mind and do it."

"Thank you. I'll try. It won't be so hard *to-morrow.*"

"Why not?"

"Oh, never mind." His face was troubled and dark as he said it.

"Percy, I shall be so glad when Jesus has made you glad."

"You take it for granted He will."

"Of course! Dear Percy, I think He will be glad too."

The bells had rung out for evening service while they were talking, and the twilight was falling. Over the western hills a stormy red rift of light showed where the sun had gone down, and the children watched it widen and glow, and then pale away into the grey, till the bells stopped and all was very still. They were still too for a little while, and then Mrs. Murray called them down to read the psalms and lessons, and sing some hymns, in which Jane was asked to join instead of sitting alone in the kitchen, while the cook, who did not mind the rain, was at church.

CHAPTER VIII.

GETTING OVER THE GROUND.

IT would be perhaps more amusing to the writer than to the reader to go on telling Bruey's daily experiences. So we will pass over the next few weeks in a few pages.

Willie Fosbery was visited nearly every week, and devoured the magazines and other books which Bruey lent him—sometimes her own, sometimes borrowed for him. She coaxed him into various other things by degrees. He never took graciously to any plan at first, but generally came round by the next week. He would not confess for some time that he had done as she wished in reading to old Mrs. Fayling, and then left her with the impression that he had been once or so, when presently Mrs. Murray brought the report that he "had been nigh every day." By the next week there was less trouble to get the truth out of him, that he had been every day, to the old woman's great comfort and delight; and it soon came to be an institution, that as soon as Mrs. Fayling, junior, had "fettled" her mother-in-law—otherwise, fed and tidied and settled her for the morning—Willie should go in and read.

Then Bruey induced him, as a personal favour and benefit to herself, to coach up the unfortunate little Bella in the verses and hymns which she taught her class, and by this extra teaching to keep her abreast of the others in her acquirements, if not in her intelligence.

"It does hinder me so sadly, Willie, having to wait for her to get them perfect," she said, quite pitifully; "I really don't know what I shall do; I shall be so very much obliged to you if you will help me, by making her learn them in the week."

What could Willie do but consent to the first request made to him by a young lady? Bruey never knew the hundreds of times the verses were repeated, while he patiently listened and prompted; nor how deeply they were thereby engraven on the cripple boy's own heart.

She bought a Bible for him out of her own money—only a tenpenny one, for her savings were not large; but in the eyes of both giver and receiver it was quite a grand present, and certainly a grand pleasure. The cost of the gift mounted up to a shilling by the addition of two penny pencils—one for general use; the other to be kept sacredly, like the one which always lay in Bruey's table-drawer, for marking the chosen verses. She arranged with him to read the same chapters that she did, both morning and evening, and the idea of "keeping level with Miss Bruey" induced him to go steadily on with what he would have tired of in a few days; while to Bruey herself it was often a help when tempted to shorten her reading, or even omit it altogether. It was a great interest, too, to see every week what verses he had marked, while he carefully looked out all her chosen verses, and treasured up the bits of paper on which she marked them day by day on purpose to bring to him.

She also brought down to him the little paper of Scripture questions or proofs which her mamma gave her every week as part of her Saturday lessons, sometimes giving him any little help or guidance to the answers, such as she had received from her mamma.

Alice Fosbery found a nursemaid's place, but *not* a perambulator. The children, little twin boys, "could walk," according to their parents, who kept a little shop; but Alice soon found that "looking after them" included a great deal of very hard work, for if they cried to be carried, carried they must be, first one and then the other. She soon found her back and arms and legs aching; and though too proud to complain for a time, was obliged to leave her place in May, and come home till another could be found. *Not* a nursemaid's place this time, if she could help it!

At school all went on pleasantly, with occasional ups and downs. Nanny Smith was troublesome, and Hetty Fosbery would talk, and Sophy Willis would fidget, but on the whole it was a dear little class, and it was quite aware that it had a dear little teacher. Mary Shelton's old hat had found its way up to Calton Terrace, and been trimmed up by Bruey herself with some old black velvet. An old doll had been turned out, and after a most delightful washing up of its clothes, and some additions to its wardrobe, which made Bruey almost inclined to take to dolls again herself, it was delivered into Sophy's hands, to whom it appeared a perfectly inexhaustible provision for all the rainy days till the end of the world. Her cares were further lightened by the fact of Jim's cough yielding to the combination of cough mixture and new shoes, so that after Easter he was able to go to the infant school.

What about Percy? If you had asked Bruey, she would probably have looked puzzled and said nothing. She was disappointed. After that Sunday evening, she rather expected to see Percy—well, she did not know quite *what,* but different. But she did not see any great difference. He did not follow her to her room again, as she half hoped and half feared. Sometimes he came down in good time, but sometimes there was an unsatisfactory tone in the "All right!" with which he acknowledged the three taps which she never forgot to give, and she felt it was not "all right." And sometimes, when he was very late, he came down looking pale and dull, and as if he had had too little instead of too much sleep, and was not at all rested and refreshed as she always felt. And on such mornings he seemed either noisy and rough, or gloomy and not happy. She prayed for him, and once or twice made little efforts to renew the Sunday evening talk, but it did not seem to answer. She could not tell her mother her little trouble about him, nor Miss Allison, whose Sunday afternoon walks home with her were a great treat, and often a great help; because it would not have been fair to tell what he had said to her, and she could not have told what she had said to him. So she had to keep her trouble and puzzle to herself; and yet not to herself, for more than once or twice she told One about it, who understood it well. And when she did this she always came away from her little praying-corner with a happy feeling that it would be "all right" in time—in *His* time.

As for herself, some things grew easier, and some harder; at least so it seemed. It was certainly easier to keep her temper. She had found this a daily temptation, and put a large T at the top of her card, which reminded her every morning to pray for grace to conquer her temper. But after the T stood a P, and this represented a more difficult matter, which turned up in such unexpected ways that she was quite surprised at herself. She was finding out that it is not only naughty actions and naughty words which prove our sinfulness and need forgiveness, but that, deep down, there are thoughts and feelings and beginnings of naughtiness, which need the precious blood of Christ to "wash away the stain" just as much. She never knew half how much there was to be forgiven till long after that blessed message came to her in the autumn twilight.

CHAPTER IX.

"A PAGE FROM IRISH HISTORY" MAKES A PAGE OF BRUEY'S HISTORY.

THE prayer of that stormy Sunday evening, that she might be shown if there were any other work for her to do, was often repeated. In one way it was constantly answered, for little things kept turning up which seemed to be the right work to do, sometimes for her mamma, sometimes for Percy, sometimes for Willie Fosbery, or her little girls. But though Bruey accepted all these as answers to her prayer, and tried to do each little thing faithfully, she still had a sort of expectation that some other answer would come, and that something else would turn up over and above all this.

And the answer did come, in an unexpected way, when the days grew long and lovely, and May was passing into June. One Saturday evening, after a late tea, Percy lay on his back on the grass-plot of the little garden, kicking, because he had pretty well exhausted himself with sundry violent games with his schoolfellows, and this was his usual mode of recruiting himself. Mrs. Murray came out with a newspaper in her hand. "Percy, you will get rheumatism if you lie on the grass like that, after you have been so hot. Get up."

He turned a somersault, and came, right side up, a little nearer to his aunt. "All square, Aunt; but what's a fellow to do? It rests one. You would find it so comfortable."

"If you please, ma'am, you are wanted," said Jane, stepping across the broad path into the garden.

"Can't you sit down on the garden seat if you are tired?" said Mrs. Murray. "Here, you can have the *Rilverton Advertiser* to look over; I must go in again."

Percy took the paper, and strolled about with it. Bruey came out and joined him. "Oh, you have got the paper!" she said, in a half-disappointed tone. For she did not care about accidents and murders, which are a boy's chief idea of the value of a newspaper.

"I shan't be long with it; there is no news that I can see." He turned over a page. "Hallo! here is a sort of a story; what's this?"

Bruey looked over his shoulder. "That looks interesting, isn't it? Won't you read it to me?"

She slipped her hand into his arm, and so evidently meant to be read to, that Percy went on without further ado, reading the article aloud as they sauntered slowly round and round about the garden path.

It was headed "A Page from Irish History," and a very interesting page Bruey thought it, but she did not know that the result of reading it would be to make a new and very pleasant page in her own little history. It was as follows:—

"A PAGE FROM IRISH HISTORY."

"It may not be generally known that about one-fourth of the population of Ireland, or rather more than a million and a half of our fellow-subjects, are Irish-speaking—that is, either totally unacquainted with English, or use it with reluctance as a disliked foreign tongue. They regard whatever is presented to them in it with distrust and prejudice, but hail the sound of their own language with a singular confidence and affection. They are accustomed to say the Irish is one of the only three tongues in the world of which the devil is not master, inasmuch as 'St. Patrick wouldn't let him learn it.' Hence it would follow that whatever is spoken in it cannot proceed from *him*.

"In years gone by, this much-loved tongue was a means of influence neglected by the Protestant Church. But at length an earnest-hearted young clergyman, the Rev. John G——, now Bishop of C——, who had preached many an eloquent sermon in the city of Dublin, resolved that his own Irish fluency should no longer be a talent unemployed. He consequently determined on a tour to the West of Ireland, there to speak for his Master in their own tongue to those who scarcely understood the Saxon speech, and to whom it was unwelcome. He came to Doonbeg, a town where an Irish Protestant sermon had never yet been delivered. After much opposition he obtained the use of the County Courts, every other door being closed against him. The news spread far and wide that a sermon in Irish would be preached on an appointed day by a gentleman from Dublin. Such a thing had never been heard of before. The ears of the priests tingled as the burst of wave after wave of the quickly-awakened excitement fell upon them; and they began to bethink themselves how this dangerous move might be met.

"They were not long in choosing an instrument well fitted for the purpose in view. A young man lived in the place, already distinguished by rare mental gifts, and also endowed with great physical strength. He was withal a zealous adherent of the Holy Roman Church, ready for anything or everything in her defence, whether by tongue or by arm. To him the priest, in his fear, addressed himself. 'Tom, my boy, you're a faithful son of the Holy Mother Church, I'm thinking?'

"'Bad luck to the spalpeen[1] that denies the same, your Reverence!'

"'There's a small job, Tom, that wants to be done by a true hand at the County Courts to-morrow, and where will I find any one, do you think?'

"Tom, who was noways dull of comprehension, 'took' immediately, answering his Reverence's insinuation with an anticipatory grin of delight, and 'I'm the boy, yer Reverence!'

"The details of the 'small job' were speedily arranged to their mutual satisfaction.

"The appointed day and hour came, and good Mr. G——, in default of a pulpit, took his post on a platform covered with green baize, in the midst of a throng of Irish excitables, whom no priestly admonitions had been able to deter from coming to hear this wonderful sermon. Denser and denser grew the crowd, pressing and pushing and packing, till retreat from any of the inner ranks became an impossibility, and the chance of obtaining silence apparently about as great as if it were requested from a bee-hive on the point of swarming! At length no more could enter, and Mr. G—— stood up to face a congregation that would have astonished a sober Saxon. One spell alone could enchain the turbulent mass, and that one he was about to exercise. He spoke: and the tones of their own musical tongue, which never fail to reach the Irish heart, glided forth like oil on the waves. Every noisy tongue was hushed, every eye fixed, as the words of God's own Book, so sweet, so new, poured through the building. Suddenly—ere even the first sentence was complete—there arose a tremendous thundering beneath the very feet of the speaker. He stopped—the thundering stopped. He continued—the thundering continued louder than ever. But above it was heard Mr. G——'s strong voice, 'Ah, Satan, I always knew you would oppose me if you could, but I did not expect you this way!' Then the hum of the great bee-hive waxed louder. 'Indeed, and it's the devil himself come to carry him off!' cried one. 'Whisht there, sure an' it's the blessed St. Patrick himself that's warnin' us not to hearken,' said another. 'Holy Virgin and St. Michael, if ye'll help me out, I'll never come in again!' exclaimed a third. Getting out being out of the question, the ejaculators had to remain, *nolens volens*,[2] to see the solution of the doubt as to whether the noise proceeded from the devil

---

[1] spalpeen: an Irish word for "rascal"   [2] Latin: perforce, forcibly

or St. Patrick! Mr. G—— was not to be outdone by any inimical power, human or fiendish. So, assuming an attitude of defiance of whatever might be beneath him, he cried out with a stentorian voice, 'You shall not be too much for me yet, Satan; we will see who can hold on the longest.'

"As the reader may conjecture, the deafening noise really proceeded from the devoted Tom, concealed under the platform; he was wielding with vigorous energy a large sledge-hammer. Mr. G——, heedless of the uproar, perseveringly went on with his sermon, waging with his voice the contest of wind *versus* muscle. The assembly grew quiet out of sheer curiosity. Mr. G——'s lungs were remarkably strong, and the sledge-hammer was remarkably heavy; and ere long the strokes of the latter became less tremendous. Then occasional rests became necessary, followed by spasmodic efforts to keep it up. Fainter and fainter grew the blows, for Tom's arm now ached terribly. Stiller grew the multitude, for Mr. G—— held on his way triumphantly. At last, nothing was to be heard but the strange and glorious story of peace, touching the hearts of those untaught hearers, sounding with trumpet clearness in their eager ears, entering with harplike sweetness into their restless souls—and all in Erin's own beautiful language!

"Three days after, the preacher was leaving Doonbeg, when a young man begged for an interview. 'That wasn't all true, your honour,' he exclaimed, 'that you said three days ago?'—'Indeed,' replied Mr. G——; 'it was true—blessed be God!'—'And how will I know that it is, then?' asked the inquirer. Offering him a book, the preacher said, 'Will you take this, and then you will know?' The book was accepted. It was an *Irish* Bible.

"Several years passed, and many more Irish sermons were preached, and many more eager listeners found, in the Emerald Isle. But the sweet story of peace had not yet been heard in the stormy and mountainous peninsula of Cleena, in the far south-west. Through the twenty miles of its rock-bound length, there was not one who knew the Word of God and its glad messages. But the Word was coming. A young clergyman, full of love and zeal, stood there at length, and preached for the first time of Redemption only through the blood of Christ.

"An uncouth congregation had assembled, rougher if anything than Mr. G——'s. Still, Irish words could entrance even them, and they crowded round the minister with their ragged hats overshadowing their rugged brows. Ere long one took his hat off, then another and another followed the example, until, before the sermon ended, every head was reverently uncovered. When the last words were spoken, there was silence, and more than one tattered sleeve was seen brushing away a tear—for the speaker had spoken from heart to heart. In deep and earnest tones one poor fellow burst forth, 'Thank ye, sir, ye've taken the hunger off us to-day!'

"Years again fled on, till the summer of 1856. A. great change had passed over Cleena. The same clergyman, young no longer, stood now on his pleasant lawn in the midst of that once benighted peninsula. Churches and schools gleamed cheerily amongst its magnificent scenery, where nothing but dreary cabins had been built before. Few were the homes where the Irish Bible was not read and known, to the shaming of many an *English* dwelling—might we not add, of many a Rilverton one too?

"But it is a 'high day' in Cleena. Again the preacher is surrounded. But he does not now see before him a herd of wild-looking, half-clothed beings, like those who listened to him when he first put his foot in beautiful sea-girt Cleena, when he might have said—

> 'All creation pleases,
> And only man is vile.'

Now, more than a hundred of her sons and daughters have assembled. They are neatly apparelled, books are in their hands, they are quiet and solemn in demeanour. The greater part are still young, and they are all candidates for confirmation—to the surprise and joy of the Bishop, who is there to lay the hand of blessing upon them. Some are the children of converts, others have themselves passed through the struggle of giving up the mistaken faith of their youth; but all are freed from the galling fetters of Popery, and all are ready to bless God for him who has been His instrument in this wonderful work.

"The inquiry cannot fail to interest us—Who is he?

"Let the priest of Doonbeg recognise the broad forehead and powerful frame of his once willing tool! Let Mr. G—— recognise his voice as that of the young man who strove not to believe what he heard, yet took the Irish Bible to 'search and look!' It is even so. Tom Brallaghan, the zealous and the bigoted, he of the strong arm and the sledge-hammer, is now the Rev. Thomas Brallaghan, the eloquent, the earnest, and the loving-one who sees even now the fruit of his many years' toil in the immense parish of which he is rector. Truly the confirmants around him are a noble harvest already, but he is still sowing and watering, and a yet richer in-gathering may be vouchsafed to him.

"Where shall we find him next? and when?

"Among ourselves, in our own ancient city of Rilverton, it is hoped, ere many more days have passed," employing his gifted warm-heartedness in the cause of the Society which sent him to the scene of his present labours, striving to awaken the sympathy of many towards his beloved country. Who will not give him the *Cead mille failthe?*"[1]

"Does that mean that the Irishman who was hammering under the platform is coming to Rilverton?" asked Bruey, when Percy had finished reading.

"I suppose so. He must be rather a brick. I should like to see him."

"So should I. But we should not know him if we met him."

"Oh, but it means that he is coming to hold forth somewhere; either a sermon, or a meeting."

"Then I hope it will be a meeting, for then mamma will go; but if it was only a sermon, it might not be at St. Mary's, and then I could not hear him."

Next day notice was given in St. Mary's, that the Rev. Thomas Brallaghan would preach two sermons in that church, God willing, on the following Sunday, on behalf of the "Irish Society." Bruey and Percy exchanged a gratified glance.

In coming out of church, they saw the notice of the said sermons in large letters, and also of a meeting to be held in the Town Hall on the following evening.

At dinner there was less Sunday-school talk than usual, as Bruey was eager to tell her mamma about the coming preacher, and to extract a promise that she might go to the meeting. Mrs. Murray did not like making promises, but after having run through a little string of objections, that it might be wet, that Bruey might have a cold, that it was sure not to be over before nine, and that was so late for Bruey, a final "Well, we will see," answered nearly as well as a promise, seeing that according to usual experience it meant much the same thing.

The week went round as usual; the sermons were preached on the Sunday; and at seven o'clock on the Monday evening, seeing that neither rain nor sore throats occurred, Mrs. Murray, Bruey, and Percy were sitting in the midst of a delightfully full meeting in the Town Hall of Rilverton, waiting for the appearance of chairman, deputation, and supporters on the platform. Percy was slightly restive. "You could have told me all about it when you came back. I should not have been gone to bed. What's the fun of stewing here for two hours?"

"O Percy, I know you will like it when it begins; of course it's stupid waiting, but it will strike seven directly, and then Mr. Brallaghan will come and speak."

"And then one won't be able even to talk! I'll do a good deal for you, Bru, but coming to meetings is more than a good deal. Be sure you don't wake me if I get a nap."

"What, and leave you to finish it out here after it is over? What a noise

[1] *Cead mille failthe* (Gaelic): a hundred thousand welcomes.

you would set up! The police might think it was a ghost. But you won't go to sleep, I know."

Percy looked round. "Let's see what ways and means there are of making one's self comfortable. Let us at least have a chance of a nap." And he found a support for one foot on a projection of the bench before him, and wriggled himself down with his head almost between his shoulders.

"O Percy, don't sit like that, it looks so!"

"Then you shouldn't have made me come. Good-night." And he pretended to go to sleep.

"There's Mr. Brallaghan!" whispered Bruey.

And the fine head and broad shoulders of the Tom Brallaghan of the sledge-hammer appeared on the platform, and a warm greeting was given by many feet and walking-sticks and parasols, to which Percy contributed as large a share as if he were perfectly delighted with the whole affair. "I can manage that part of the business," he whispered. "Aunt, you give me a poke when he says something first-class, and I'll wake up and give him the clapping. Pretty hard, for fear I should not wake quick enough."

The speech was very interesting, especially when the introduction was over and the speaker grew warm and earnest. There was very little but what Bruey could thoroughly understand and follow, while the greater part woke all her interest, and made her give little pokes at Percy; not to waken him, as that was not necessary, but to let him know how much she liked what was being said. Percy forgot after a while to pretend to be sleepy, or to find it slow.

Mr. Brallaghan told much of the work of the old Irish Society, the oldest of all the many efforts to do good to poor Ireland. How it taught many thousands of poor Irish, who could not speak a word of the hated English tongue, to read the Bible in their own beloved tongue, and to repeat much of it by heart, so that it could never be taken away from them. How its Irish-speaking teachers went where no others were of any use. How many poor miserable creatures were made glad by the good tidings of great joy, who never heard the good news till the Irish Society sent it. How many more heard of it, and sent messages that they would like to learn to read the Book, and how very often the Irish Society had not money enough to send them a teacher, and had to say "No!" Bruey wished she could send some money to help them in providing more teachers, and more Bibles and portions. She fumbled for the sixpence in her pocket, with a very groundless hope that it might prove to be a shilling.

Then the speaker, after many interesting stories of the Irish teachers and scholars, told his hearers that it only cost five shillings to have one poor Irish person taught to read.

Only five shillings! Oh, if she had that much! But the amount in her money-box at home was about fifteen pence half-penny, which was not half enough. There were all these poor people knowing nothing about Jesus, very poor, and full of terror when ill and dying, and no one doing anything for them except the Irish Society, and that not able to teach all who would like to be taught, just for want of more five shillings! It would take weeks and months to make that sum up out of her twopence a week, and who ever liked having to wait months to give what they would like to give that minute? It was a very hopeless, long-faced view of it, not much brightened even when the speaker suggested that those who could not give much should pray. She wanted to *do* something as well as that, and she went off into such a maze of calculations and wishes on the subject, that she hardly listened to the Chairman's short closing speech, till the words "Miss Allison" startled her into attention. She had lost part of the sentence, but it was clear that Miss Allison had "kindly consented" to do something, and what followed was plain enough. "Will be very happy to supply collecting cards and papers to any one who will apply for them at No. 16, Calton Terrace." And then some half-earnest, half-playful words were added about the "power of sixpences," which in the case of one great society is calculated to be a twenty-thousand-pound power every year.

Percy thought Bruey must be very tired as they walked home, for she was not to be roused by any amount of teasing on the subject of the meeting, but went along gravely and silently; so he at last left her to her own cogitations, and chattered to his aunt.

She was full of the idea of sixpences. That was a very come-at-able coin, and it only took ten to make up a five shillings. Only persuade her mamma to let her ask Miss Allison for a card, and she felt pretty sure she could get one Irishman taught to read the Bible. She thought over the whole list of her acquaintances, and reckoned up probable sixpences and possible shillings, and imagined how she should manage to ask this one, and how she should get at the other. No wonder she had so much thinking to do that there was no room for talking. And thinking aloud would not do at this stage of the proceedings, or she would have heard plenty from Percy about "counting chickens," and it would not be pleasant to have any doubts thrown upon the hatching.

The supper was a very hurried one, for half-past nine was very late for her, and she thought it would not be a favourable moment to ask about the card. But it was too much to wait till the morning, so she asked, and, to her great delight, obtained permission, when her mamma came upstairs.

About twelve o'clock next day Miss Allison sat in her dining-room making up some accounts, when the servant announced "Miss Murray."

After a kind greeting and a kiss, Bruey said, "Mamma says I may have a card and collect sixpences for the Irish Society. I know I can get five shillings, and I may get more. Will you give me one to-day?"

"Suppose I say I will not give you one at all?"

Bruey looked astonished, but not dismayed. She was sure Miss Allison was only in fun.

"Quite true! I will not give you one at all, Bruey. There, now! you have come to the wrong person. What is to be done?"

"I don't know," said Bruey. "Dr. Carnegie said you would."

"He said no such thing!"

"I wasn't asleep!" said Bruey, laughing.

"Well, you have come to the right place, and now I will take you to the right person. You know I am only Miss Elizabeth Allison. *Miss* Allison will be delighted to give you a card. Come with me."

She led Bruey to a pleasant little sitting-room, with a large couch which could be raised or lowered to suit the invalid who lay upon it.

A sweet face smiled up from it as they entered. It was not a very old face, but soft grey hair lay upon the brow, and made it look much older than the handsome likeness of it which Miss Elizabeth Allison possessed, though there was no great difference in age.

"This is the Irish secretary," she said, leading Bruey towards her sister. "Margaret, here is your first applicant for an Irish card. She means to get five shillings at least."

Miss Allison looked as pleased as if the promise were five pounds; and felt so too. It was not much that she could do, but she could write a few notes, and keep the accounts of what might be done for the Irish Society in Rilverton; and Miss Elizabeth was very willing to undertake any walking which might be necessary in the cause. And she thought she could explain the work, and keep up the interest of any who would take a collecting card. But would any one come? She was afraid to hope much, for she was not very hopeful at any time; and there were lines on the white brow which told of suffering enough to make her take a gloomy view of everything. She had been praying that morning that God would send her some little token to show that she was right in undertaking to be Irish secretary, and that the meeting of the night before might stir up some to collect and many to give. And here was a very unexpected collector come to offer herself. Was it not an answer and a token for good? She would take it as such, and try to go on more hopefully.

So Bruey was herself a little bodily answer to prayer that morning, without having the least idea of it. She did not guess how poor suffering Miss Allison would softly "thank God and take courage" as soon as she went away. Miss Elizabeth left her with her sister, and then Miss Margaret gave her a pretty little bright green card, like a book, with spaces for thirty names, and wrote upon it, under "Collector's Name," "Miss E. B. Murray." Then she gave her some little books, also green, and showed her that they contained accounts of what was being done by the Irish teachers, and told her that it would be a good plan if she would read them through herself, and put a pencil mark against anything which she thought very interesting, because then people would look to see what was marked if they had not time to read much of the book. Then she told her a few things which she might try and remember to say, if any one asked her to explain what the Irish Society was, and what they wanted the money for; so simply put, that Bruey thought it would be quite easy to tell to every one. Before she went away, Miss Allison thanked her so warmly that she was quite surprised, and wondered why she seemed to be so glad that she had come for a card.

CHAPTER X.

FILLING THE CARD.

"Mamma, you will give me sixpence, won't you?"

"You forget that I went to the meeting last night, and gave all I meant to give."

"Oh, but just sixpence, Mamma."

"I had much better not give you sixpence to begin with, or the next person will be less likely to give you a shilling. Wait till you can find somebody to start the card with a shilling."

"Then would not you start it with a shilling?"

"I did not mean that! But I cannot give you anything just now; I have not my purse."

Bruey went up to her own money-box. Yes, fifteen-pence-halfpenny, that was all. Percy's birthday was coming the week after next, and she would like to spend sixpence on a present for him. But two more weekly twopences would fall in by that time, so she could take out the shilling safely, and leave three-pence-halfpenny in. But she did not like to put her own name first on the card, though here was the shilling. So she wrote in the first space—

					s.	d.
A. B. C.,	.	.	.	.	1	0

That was quite appropriate for a beginning. She went down again. "Mamma, might I fetch your purse?"

"Very well. I see I shall have no peace till this is settled."

As she came down with it in her hand Percy came in.

"Just the very person I wanted! I am sure you will help me; do look here, Percy, I know you will give me sixpence for this." And she showed him the green card coaxingly.

"So you have got your card, have you? and now you think you have got me! A. B. C.! I had better go in for the next three letters, and be D. E. F. It's the only way to escape you."

"Too late now, because you owned to having heard. But be D. E. F. on the card, by all means, if you like."

"Seriously, Bruey, I don't see how I can give any more. I gave a threepenny-bit last night. It's getting near the holidays, and that means low in the pocket, and I can't ask for any more."

"Oh, I know you can give me sixpence. You would bring home sixpenny-worth of sweets or more between now and the breaking-up, and share them with me, and that's very kind of you; but I would rather you gave me sixpence for the Irish Society instead."

Percy hesitated.

"Come! I know you will, that's a good Percy!"

"Always got to knock under! Who's A. B. C., Bruey? Is it good company for me?"

"Never you mind!"

"It's you, I know, else you would tell me. What did you go and put a shilling for? it makes D. E. F. look so small. Well, I suppose I must submit to the extortion."

They came into the dining-room, and Percy executed an elaborate D. E. F. in old English for the adornment of the card.

"What an idiot I am!" he said, as he looked admiringly at his performance; "I might have got off with threepence after all, or fourpence at the outside, but it would look mean after those grand letters."

"Of course it would!" said Bruey, cutting a small caper of delight.

"So, you see," said Percy, whining and drawling, "I'm afraid I shall have to be extravagant, and match A. B. C. with a shilling!"

"Oh you dear good boy! Now I did not really ever think you were going to do that! Mamma, only fancy, Percy has given me a shilling, and I never asked for anything but sixpence!"

"Now see what you have brought *me* into, Percy! You spoil that child. Here! here is your shilling."

Three shillings! This looked like getting on. By dinner-time there were five names on the card, for Cook gave sixpence and Jane threepence. Bruey had a private plan for the afternoon, but Mrs. Murray said, "When it gets cooler I am going down to Gilling's Yard, and you may come with me if you choose."

She had not seen Willie the week before, so it would be three weeks if she waited till next week, and Willie would be looking out for her. Would it be kind and right to disappoint him? It was a little struggle, for she liked doing at once whatever her head was full of; but she decided to go to Gilling's Yard, and hope for to-morrow for Irish Society work.

She found him sitting in his little chair outside the door, and his brightened look as she came up quite repaid her for the small self-denial. There was plenty to communicate, a paper of texts to exchange, and the new hymn for Bella to be found, and Willie's opinion of a book to be heard. After this, as there was no need for Bruey to follow her mamma into the houses, she told him about Tom Brallaghan and the sledge-hammer, and how she had heard him speak last night, and what he told about the Irish Society, and the poor Irish being taught to read their own Bible. How Bruey's report would have looked if it had been taken down in shorthand and printed, we cannot say; but how it sounded to Willie was quite another matter. To him it was not merely as good, but much better than a book, when Miss Bruey told him about anything she had heard or read.

"So now, Willie," she concluded, quite confidentially, "I have a collecting-card, and I am going to ask all my friends for sixpences; and I am quite sure I shall get enough for one to be taught to read, and very likely two; and perhaps—only think!—*perhaps* three!"

"What is a collecting card?" asked Willie.

She took the little green card-book out of her pocket, and showed it as if it were a new treasure. Willie examined it in much the same light.

"You get silver."

"Yes; but I shall get copper too. Look, one of our servants gave three-pence."

"I couldn't get silver, but I might get coppers. Would they give me a card for coppers?"

What a charming idea! Bruey did not stay to consider how, when, or where poor Willie was to get halfpence, and the smallness of the probable amount no more affected her pleasure than it had Miss Allison's; it was so delightful for Willie to have a card, and share her work and her enjoyment of it. She knew, too, that anything which gave him something to do or to think about did him great good. So she assured him that Miss Allison would give her a card for him, and arranged that Hetty should come up for it next morning; and then she related to him the simple details which she had learnt from Miss Allison for the information of inquirers on the subject. The whole business was more satisfactory and delightful than if anybody had given her a whole half-crown; and her face was simply radiant when, on reaching Calton Terrace that evening, she went on to the end house, and sent in a message to ask "if Miss Allison would kindly give her another card for a little boy who could only collect halfpence."

Next day, with mamma's permission, some more serious collecting began. It was rather alarming, but it was not Bruey's way to leave any possible stones unturned. So, after lessons were over, she went, armed with her card and some little books and papers, to No. 1 of the Terrace, and rang the bell. She did not venture an assault upon the knocker.

"Will you please give this to Mr. and Mrs. Smith?" she said to the servant.

"They are not in," was the reply; "can you leave it?"

"No, thank you, I will call again."

She went to No. 2. Three old ladies lived here; surely *one* would give her sixpence. She had written in her best hand, on a tiny sheet of note-paper,—"Miss E. B. Murray will be very much obliged if any kind friend will give sixpence to the Irish Society"; and this was laid inside the card.

"Are the Miss Morrises in?"

"Yes, miss—will you walk in?"

"No, thank you; but will you please give them this, and I will wait and see if there is any answer?"

She stood, smiling and trembling, and tantalised beyond endurance at the length of time the servant remained away, and the occasional words she caught through the half-open dining-room door. They must be looking all through the little book and paper she had sent in with the card, and perhaps they would be quite interested and send her out sixpence apiece, or even a shilling apiece! At last the servant came back, and handed the card and book to Bruey, saying "the Miss Morrises always gave at church, and never gave when people came round."

Poor Bruey! Would it be all like this? How dreadful! They *might* have given just sixpence! So they might, Bruey; and I would not give much for the faith and charity of one who cannot find a sixpence for a little collector. It is not begging, but work, and very hard work too, and very well worth a little sympathising addition to the card. And collectors, young or old, would always rather have the smallest coin as a mere expression of real sympathy than be turned away quite empty-handed. She walked a little way back towards the entrance-gate of the terrace before she could get up courage enough to try No. 3; and a little prayer rose up, swiftly and silently, through the June sunshine, to the unseen golden gates beyond. She stood some time at No. 3 before the servant answered the bell, and then received the pleasing information that the family had gone to the seaside the day before.

Oh dear! Even the green card seemed to have grown dingy. Should she miss No. 4, and go on to No. 5, where she knew the people a little, and had a better chance? That would be cowardly; she would try once more. And a few words came into her mind, like a cool, sweet breeze—"*As I was with Moses, so will I be with thee.*" Moses had no collecting-card certainly, but managing all those children of Israel was much worse, she thought, and God helped him wonderfully all the while, and so He would help her. Wonderfully too, perhaps.

A good-natured-looking old gentleman lived at No. 4, and Bruey had often watched him set off with a white-haired lady for a little walk, with a devoted black dog behind them, which they called "Derry." This was an Irish name, so it might dispose them to do something for the Irish Society.

She sent in her card. Talk about suspense! People who never worked a collecting card with proper energy do not know what collectors endure in that line while standing on the door-steps, or at best on the mat in the hall.

The servant came back, and said, "Will you walk in, miss? Master would like to speak to you."

This was very awful, and yet very hopeful. She went in, and found old Mr. Nelson with her card in his hand, and old Mrs. Nelson with her book and paper. "How do you do, little lady?" he said. "We know each other by sight, I think."

Bruey shook hands with both. Derry got up, walked round her, sniffed, and lay down again, considering the inspection satisfactory. He evidently approved of the Irish Society.

"So you are a collector for the Irish Society?"

"Yes," said Bruey, with a sigh and a dismal look.

"You do not find it very lively work, do you?"

"Not yet, but I do hope I shall get more soon. I shall go on till I do."

"Well done! Now, if you will tell me what it is all about, perhaps I will give you something."

Bruey tried to recollect her lesson from Miss Allison, but it had all melted away, and she could not imagine how to begin.

"It is for the Irish Society!" was all she could find to say.

"Are you quite sure the Irish Society does not mean Fenians? Those dreadful people, you know, who would cut all the Saxons' throats if they dared. It would be a shocking business to collect for them, and I don't think I could subscribe unless you satisfy my mind on that point."

Though this attack was obviously in fun, and Bruey never supposed the old gentleman really thought her in league with the Fenians, it answered the purpose of unloosing her tongue, and she roused into a warm denial of the connection, and that led easily on to telling what the work was, and why it was so much needed.

Mr. Nelson seemed amused, and asked her several questions; and though not always sure which were in earnest and which in fun, she got through this new catechism pretty well. At last he said, "But you can't expect me to give twice over to the same thing, and I must tell you I do subscribe to the Irish Church Missions."

"It is the same *sort* of thing, but indeed it is not the *same* thing; so perhaps you would give a little to this too."

"Then you must show me the difference."

"Oh, I wish I could tell it you like Miss Allison told me! But I think it is this. The one goes to the people who know English, and the other goes to the poor, out-of-the-way people who don't know it at all, and hate the sound of it. And the one has great meetings and classes in large towns to argue with the Roman Catholics, and show them how mistaken they are; while the other tries to teach the people to read the Irish Bible, and to learn it by heart, and see how sweet and beautiful it is. So one is wanted most for one part of Ireland, and the other most for the other part. Miss Allison said we don't want any one to give to the Irish Society *instead* of to the Irish Church Missions, but to give it a little as *well;* because they are both doing different parts of the same work, and neither of them can do just what the other does."

"Very good!" said Mr. Nelson. "I really think we have fairly earned a contribution, have we not, Grandmamma?"

Mrs. Nelson did not disagree with this; and now came the reward.

"Constance, can you find me a pen that will write?" asked Mr. Nelson, addressing a young lady who sat at work by the window. She brought one, and looked over his shoulder as he slowly laid the card open on the table, and prepared to write his name.

"How much are you going to give, Grandpapa?"

"How much are you?" he replied.

"That is not fair, Grandpapa; it is you who were asked, not myself."

Bruey caught at the straw of possibility, and looked up so pleadingly with a soft, "Oh! would you really?" that Miss Constance did not feel inclined to resist, and said so. "Oh, how *very* nice!" said Bruey. "That fills up another line in my card. There are three pages, and ten lines in each, and I do so want to fill as many as I can."

This was grand success; Mr. Nelson put down two shillings, and then passed the card to the old lady, saying, "There, Grandmamma, I thought two from me and one from you would do better than one half-crown."

Then Miss Constance took the card and wrote her name, saying, "I shall only give sixpence; I'm very poor, Grandpapa; but I don't see why Isabel should escape, so I shall put down sixpence for her too, and she can refund it when she comes in. Now, Miss Murray, you have only one line to fill, to finish the page."

"I wish all the houses were like this!" cried Bruey, overflowing.

The good-byes were accompanied with good wishes, and she went out of the house convinced that collecting was a most beautiful occupation, and with very much enlarged ideas of the sum total to be paid in to the secretary.

At No. 5 lived Mrs. Madingley, a young mother with four little dots, of whom only two could walk, and not one could speak in a tongue understood by ordinary people. Mr. Madingley was away all day, so Bruey's expectations rested on the lady. She was at work upon some diminutive garments, and went on with them as soon as she had shaken hands.

"My dear Bruey," she said, when she had heard all that was to be said for the Irish Society, "the very idea of coming to me! My purse might have a hole at each end, the money runs out so fast. Babies can't be dressed for nothing, and sixpences and shillings are wanted in all directions. You should go to the young ladies who don't know what to do with their pocket money." Bruey would have liked a list of such persons; but Mrs. Madingley went on. "You don't know what things cost. Look at this bit of Valenciennes; that is sixteenpence a yard, and a yard goes no way. And one can't trim the dear little creatures' things with nasty common rubbish, you know." Bruey didn't know, but of course Mrs. Madingley did. "And shoes! Why, Bruey, I bought a tiny little pair of blue shoes for Lina yesterday, and they cost five shillings, such lovely little things; and they will be all rubbed out at the toes in a fortnight, and then what am I to do? Don't you see that it won't do at all for me to give all my money away, and let the pretty darlings go barefoot?"

Of course it would not; but though Bruey felt there was a flaw somewhere in the argument, she thought it would not be polite to argue against the babies. So she tried a counter-appeal to sympathy. She could see that Mrs. Madingley was quite untouched by the needs of the far-off Irish, and that her representations had entirely failed. It would have been ten times nicer if she would have sympathised in the least with the cause; but failing that, Bruey did not see why it should suffer practically for her indifference. So she tried another tack. "O Mrs. Madingley! if people would only give me a penny it would be better than nothing;—or sixpence," she added, lest she might be taken at her word. "You don't know how dreadful it is to call at three houses running, and get nothing."

"Then what do you do it for?"

Yes, what did she do it for? She paused, and smiled. It was true enough that the motive was mixed up with a great desire to get as many lines of her card filled as possible, and to have the pleasure of taking much more than was expected to Miss Allison; but she honestly felt that this was *not* all, nor nearly all, the reason. Mrs. Madingley had set several stitches before the reply to her question came. "Because I *do* want those poor Irish to know about Jesus Christ, and be happy."

Mrs. Madingley glanced up from her work. Words, tone, and look were too serious to be answered very lightly. "What a strange child you are!" was all she said. There was a pause, which Bruey did not know how to fill up. She would not have cared to try if she had known that her answer had woke up an old feeling in the busy young mother's heart, and a wish that she were like this strange child, and like others who did "know about Jesus Christ, and were happy."

While Bruey sat wondering what would come next, and whether she had better go, her eye fell on the chimney-piece, and on a little pile of halfpence on the corner of it. She nearly made Mrs. Madingley prick her finger by her sudden exclamation, "Oh, would you not give me those halfpence, or some of them! I should so like to have them, because if people saw a queer sum down on my card, perhaps they would give me the halfpence off their chimney-pieces too, instead of nothing."

This rather novel request could not well be refused. "But I won't have my name down, Bruey. You must put 'A Friend,' or something of that sort. If you once have your name down for anything, there's no end to it."

Bruey considered, and then her eyes lighted up with glee. "I know! No, I won't put 'A Friend'; I like something fresh. We will have '*Off the Chimney-piece*—7½d.' Do write it. Very plain, please, so that people can't help reading it when I send in my card."

At No. 6, where lodgings were let, the card was sent down from the drawing-room without any acknowledgment or message whatever. "I was afraid you would not get anything from those folks, Miss Murray. The old gentleman grumbles over every bit he puts into his mouth, and the ladies are just as bad; and yet I'm sure they have the best of everything, and their keep costs as much in a week as had ought to do for a month. And *I* ought to know, that was housekeeper ten years before I married. That's the gentry that never have nothing to spare for anything good."

"I wish they only knew what Mr. Brallaghan told us about the poor Irish, and how they sometimes walk twenty miles to hear the Irish missionaries without anything to eat. Only fancy being very ill, and ever so afraid to die, and nobody to tell one anything about how to go to heaven or comfort one, except in, say—Spanish! wouldn't it be sad, Mrs. Brown? But it is like that with these poor Irish in the far west and south; they can't speak English, so unless the

Irish Society goes to them, they have to die in the dark, without ever hearing about—about—the Lord Jesus being the Way to heaven," she concluded, in a low tone.

"I am sure it's very good of young ladies like you to collect for them; I know you don't always get much for your trouble; and it's generally them as has the most as gives the least."

"Would *you* give me something, Mrs. Brown?"

"Well, miss, I should be very glad to, if I was able; but we have been rather unfortunate in our rooms this winter, and I have to mind it does not go out faster than it comes in. And we do subscribe to the missionary, and to the schools."

"Oh, I did not mean grand subscriptions like that! I meant if you would give sixpence or so, or even threepence. See, I have had one threepenny-bit already. And if *everybody* gave me sixpence, it would soon run up to a great deal."

"Oh dear, miss, I did not know you took such small amounts; I'm sure I shall be most happy if you will kindly take it, and excuse more. I shan't miss sixpence, so you are very welcome to that."

Mrs. Brown was thoroughly pleased to give her sixpence, when she found it would be appreciated.

Percy had come back from school, and was waylaying his cousin as she came out of No. 6. "How have you got on?" he said.

"Please don't hinder me," was her reply. "I know it is nearly dinner-time, and I do so want to finish the houses on this side of ours first. I don't know how long they may keep me at No. 7."

"I'll come and knock for you."

"Oh! please don't; I know you will make such a tremendous noise, and then I should feel quite ashamed if I had to go in. Don't tease me now; do let me alone till I have finished. I did not mean to be cross; indeed, it is only that I am in such a hurry."

He whistled, and walked off.

"Will you kindly take this in to Mrs. Arthur," she said to the servant at No. 7, "and I will wait for an answer?"

It was short work here, for the servant returned in a minute or two with the card, and a sixpence on it. Not much, but very easily earned this time, thought Bruey. She was not sorry, for she was hot and tired, and it was pleasant to go in with the silver tinkling in her pocket, and the second page of her card begun, and take off her hat, and rest, and feel she had done what she could. The dinner-bell rang in a few minutes.

"How flushed you are!" said Mrs. Murray.

"The sun is so hot to-day, Mamma; but I feel quite cool now."

"I ought not to have let you go out in the heat, tiring yourself. You go and lie down after dinner for a good hour; you can begin your practising a little later."

"O Mamma! if you don't mind, I would so much rather begin my lessons at the usual time, and get done; I did so want to do some more houses this afternoon."

"No, dear, not on any account. You won't do anything before tea except prepare your lessons; and if you like to go out, you will go in the garden, and keep in the shade."

This was quite wise and kind, and Bruey submitted with a pretty good grace. At dinner she retailed her experiences of the morning.

"I think you have done pretty well," said Mrs. Murray. "Grown-up people get more refusals than children."

"Let's look!" said Percy. "Why, you have seven names out of seven houses! I hear my mother talking about collecting for some Jews, or Gentiles, or something, and she would think it was the millennium if she could fill up her card at that rate."

"But," said Bruey, gravely, "there's this whole afternoon that I must not get anything! I wish it were not hot. O Percy!"——

"How you made me jump! It's dangerous to startle one that way. Suppose I had had my knife in my mouth!"

"But you never have. And I have such a good idea. My card will be lying idle all this afternoon; now, would not you take it to school with you, and see if some of the boys would not give you something? Halfpence would do."

Percy laughed loudly. "I should just like to see myself collecting! It would take a very big telescope to see it, though, it's so far off. Aunt, are you sure Bruey isn't just a little bit demented?"

"You know I always leave you two to fight your own battles," she answered, looking rather amused.

"Percy, you know I am not demented, not one bit. And it is just what I should like to see—you collecting. It would be as easy again for you as for me; because you are older and cleverer, and you can talk better."

"Oh!—well!—query!" said he, rolling up his eyes.

"Please don't interrupt. There is Alfred Ellerson,—(Mamma, you remember how nice he was that evening he came to tea with Percy),—I am sure he would give sixpence, if you ask him, and tell him I shall be very much obliged to him."

"That's possible, certainly. He was rather smitten, I believe, Aunt; so that's not a bad shot of Bruey's."

She took no notice of this, but went on. "And the two Arranbrookes, one of them would surely give some thing, if it was but twopence. I can't think of any one else, except Stirling, and you said he was a stingy fellow, but he might give something. I wish I knew the rest. Stay, I'll tell you;—don't you remember telling me one day, when you were talking reasonably, that Scott, the head boy, was such a good fellow, and you thought he was 'quite religious' you said; now, if you would ask him, that would make four."

"Talk of impositions! where's anything to equal this young person, Aunt? Don't you call *this* imposition with a vengeance? Worse than lines, any day!"

Bruey never allowed the shadow of a doubt upon the certainty that Percy would come round to whatever she wished; and this calm confidence partly amused and partly provoked him, but very seldom failed to be effectual. And so it came to pass that when Bruey went upstairs to lie down, the green card went down to Rilverton in Percy's pocket.

She had a book, but it was one she had read before, so she was not much absorbed in it, and part of the hour was spent in further scheming and calculating. If Uncle Joseph would but come and fetch Percy at midsummer, that would be certainly another shilling. But this was not likely. Could she write to him, and send him her card? That would do; but meanwhile the collecting would be at a standstill. Possibly Miss Allison would give her another card, on due explanation; and then one could be kept going at home, while the other made little journeys by post. And she would not need to write much; there was enough on the card itself to explain matters. This opened quite a wide field, for she thought of at least four persons to whom she could send it, and perhaps more than one in each house would add a little.

When she came down, she communicated this plan to her mother, and asked if she might go and ask for another card.

"My dear, I can't let you go teasing Miss Allison so often. She won't like it. You forget what an invalid she is. Every one will be tired to death of the Irish Society if you go on like this. Now go to your music, if you are quite rested."

So she practised, and then took her lessons out into the garden to prepare. It was cooler and pleasanter than in the house, upon which the afternoon sun was beginning to tell. She finished them long before tea-time, and then went on with her story-book, listening every now and then for Percy, who was nearly due. A step sounded on the gravel; she looked up, though it came from the wrong direction, and her eye met Miss Elizabeth Allison's. "Bruey!" She ran to the little gate, and stood under the shadow of a laburnum with her friend.

"How nice! I did so want to see you. Do you think your sister would give me another card?"—and she explained why she wanted it.

"You don't want it this minute, I suppose? My sister is resting; these warm days try her sadly; but when I come back I will bring or send you one with pleasure."

"Then I am glad I did not come for it. Thank you very much."

She went in to tell her mamma, and to wash her hands before tea. Percy was late, which was trying. At last he came. "Are you not glad to see me, Bru? That's one advantage of not being punctual. Well, I couldn't help it."

"Where is my card? It was very good of you to take it. Did Stirling give you anything?"

"Stirling give me anything? Let me see; well, yes, I recollect. He gave me a good rattling box on the ear once; and a kick another time, I think, but that I'm not sure about. I can't produce the gifts, because I gave them back. But you can take my word."

"Now, Percy! Do tell me, because I want to know. For my card, I mean."

"Now, was I likely to take anything for your card, when you did not authorise me to sell it?"

"The only comfort is that I do not think you would go on in this way if you had nothing for me. *Do* tell me."

"Tell you what?"

"What have you got on my card."

"Oh! that is another question. Yes, there is something on it—a blot. I'm very sorry, Bru. I'll get it out beautifully with my ink-erasor."

"Have you not kept me on thorns long enough yet? Now! *Do* tell me!"

"Patience is a virtue; but it does not seem to be 'its own reward' to you. Come, then, here is your card. I did ask Stirling; but he is a stingy little dog, so I knew it would be no use. But another fellow heard me chaffing him about it, and wanted to know what the row was, so he let himself in for it, for I charged him threepence for the information, and he put down 'Virtuous Indignation— 6d.'"

"I'm very much obliged both to you and him for the sixpence; but I wish he had not written that, it will look so odd."

"All the better, I should say. Anything to make your card an interesting document. Then Scott forked out a shilling, and said he liked to encourage beggars of that sort. I could not possibly ask the Arranbrookes; I should never have heard the last of it, in more ways than one; but it was safe ground with Ellerson, so I tackled him, putting it all to your account; and I managed it so well that he fumbled out a shilling; but he would not put his own name down, so I put him down as 'Tomtit'; only in pencil, so you can rub it out if you like. And—stop a bit—here's threepence-halfpenny from young Williams. He was turning out his purse for some transaction about a cricket-ball with Ford, and little Goldring ran against him, and jerked it out of his hand, and sent the money flying. I helped him to pick it all up, and told him he ought to give me a commission on the job, and told him what for. He wouldn't hand over any silver, but I made him lighten his purse of the coppers for you."

Bruey's exceeding gratification was compensation to Percy, who well deserved her thanks. In the evening a few more houses were called at, so that Calton Terrace was nearly finished.

It was too near midsummer to need any candle or gas at Bruey's bedtime, and the soft, clear twilight was enough even for her evening chapter, though the brightness of the sunset was no longer opposite the window, but had shifted away to the far north-west.

She was not inclined to hurry, and before kneeling down sat for a little while curled up on her box, resting her arms on the ledge of the window. If "means of grace" meant anything that helped people to pray and be thoughtful, she thought her box and her window, and the sunsets and the sweet twilights, were undoubtedly "means of grace." So she sat and mused over the day. "*Then what do you do it for?*" The words came back to her, as she recalled her chimney-piece success at No. 5. "What for?" She had answered that, and truly; but the word seemed to change itself into "*Who* for?" Never mind about the grammar; this was how the question came into her mind, and so this is how we write it down, "*Who for?*" And an answer followed it, which made such music in her heart, that its echo glided out in a quiet whisper, and left a smile upon her lips as it passed—"*For* HIM!" Yes, really for *Him*. What did it matter if she was a little tired, and if she had trembled a little as she rang the door-bells, and more still as she tried to explain *why* the money was wanted? It was all for Him, and He had given her this nice opportunity of really doing something for Him, though she was only a little girl of twelve years old. How pleasant! He had answered the frequent Sunday-evening prayer, that He would show her if there was anything else she could do for Him; and now she would try to show Him how gratefully she accepted the answer, by doing her very best. And here was another proof that He really did hear her, and "meet" her in her little praying corner. She had not doubted it, but it was very sweet and helpful to have a new proof of it; and surely this was one.

Then her thoughts leaped back to last midsummer. It was different then. She had sat on her box, and leant on her window-ledge, and watched the sunset; but oh! so differently! Afraid to think of Him whose Name was now so sweet; afraid, shudderingly afraid, as the thought crossed her mind that sunsets would not go on for ever, and that a great day would come when the heavens would be on fire, and the earth would be burnt up. Sad, when the "beautiful gates of the sunset" reminded her of the "Pilgrim's Progress" and the Celestial City; so sad, that she tried to put away such thoughts altogether, and to forget all about them as she brushed her hair. And now? What could she do but kneel down and thank the blessed Saviour, who had not left her to wander on the dark mountains, but had called her, and drawn her with His love and kindness, and made, as she had told Percy, "almost everything seem different!" After her loving thanksgiving came little petitions that He would help her in her new work, and make people inclined to give, and that He would help her to think of persons to ask, and give her the right words to say when she tried to explain about it. Then she prayed that Willie Fosbery might be helped too. Then that Percy, dear good-natured Percy, might be blessed for having been so kind in helping her, and that some day he might love the Lord Jesus so much that he might wish to work for Him, and not merely to oblige her. Then she stopped to think what a grand thing it would be if he really wished this, because he would be able to do so much more than she could even now, and how *very* much more when they grew older! Would not God grant her even this, as He had so graciously heard her for herself?

As she lay down that night, she thought, "I wonder what will be the next work He will give me to do!" Harder work than collecting, perhaps, dear Bruey!

CHAPTER XI.

FURTHER EXPERIENCES.

THURSDAY morning of what Percy called the "Irish week!"

At breakfast Mrs. Murray said, "You may come down into the town with me directly after breakfast, Bruey, and leave your lessons till we come back; I must go, and it is too hot to start after your lessons."

"Mamma, if you don't mind, might I not stay and finish the other houses instead?"

"No, my dear; I wish Miss Benson to see you with that blue frock on before she makes your new one. I must explain to her about the sleeves, else she will make you look like an old woman. And if you are still in such a fever about your card, I daresay she would give you sixpence, but you are not to ask for more, mind."

This was enough to alter the case entirely, and she put on her hat with great alacrity. The Calton Terrace houses would not run away before evening.

On the way they stopped at the butcher's.

"Very nice little shoulder, ma'am. Leg, ma'am, would you prefer? Beautiful condition! How many pounds? I'll weigh it, ma'am, if you please."

Not at all interesting to Bruey. She caught sight of a curly-headed three-year-old peeping round the half-open door of the parlour behind the shop, and presently the little peeper toddled through it.

"Johnnie, my dear, don't go into the shop; come back to Mamma!" said a voice within. As the call was not instantly heeded, the butcher's wife followed it up by coming out and catching the little truant, who was pre-occupied with making shy advances to Bruey. "Good morning, Miss—Miss Murray, I believe. You'll excuse me calling the little man, Miss; but I did not know any one was taking notice of him, and I'm always afraid of his getting hold of a chopper when no one is looking. Would you please to take a seat, Miss, till your mamma is ready?"

"Thank you!" said Bruey; "but she won't be long. What a nice little parlour! O Mrs. Howcutt! I wonder if you would like to help a very good thing that is being done for the poor Irish in the far west, who cannot speak English? I think you would if you knew. It is only sixpences that I am asking for, and yet it will do such wonderful good."

"Bruey, I'm ready!" called Mrs. Murray.

She went quickly out to her mamma, and said, in a low tone, but with bright eyes, "Might I stay just two or three minutes longer, and overtake you at the next shop you are going to?"

"Very well; I am going to Chilton, the draper; but don't keep me waiting."

She came back to the parlour. "I was sorry to run away so suddenly."

"Oh! don't name it, Miss."

"Well, I was going to tell you about these sixpences. These poor Irish cannot read the Bible, and have none to read, if they could, and there is no one to teach them. But by this Society, which I am collecting for, three thousand are being taught every year. And those who are taught in this way know better than to make riots and disturbances, like the other Irish do; and a great many of them learn to care for it, and try to teach it to the rest."

"That's very good, Miss," said Mr. Howcutt, who had come close to the open door, and overheard the appeal. "I'll warrant that answers better in the long run than the police. The police don't seem to do much more than catch them when the mischief's done,—shooting or murdering, or what not,—and not always that! This plan of yours shuts the door before the steed is stolen."

Bruey told him a little about Mr. Brallaghan. "Yes, wife and I read that in the paper about him; and I'd a good mind to have gone, but we could not make it convenient."

"I think Mrs. Howcutt was going to give me sixpence for the Society, Mr. Howcutt; you will not forbid her, I am sure!"

"I'll give you one myself, too, with the greatest of pleasure," he replied.

So Mr. and Mrs. Howcutt figured on the card for sixpence each.

Mrs. Murray had not finished her purchases at Chilton's; Bruey stood waiting at the door for a minute, and then came to the counter.

"Mamma, might I not just go and show my card to Mr. Bainbrigge, the grocer. It is only next door but one, and he looks so good-natured."

Off she went, and another sixpence was the result. The shop between was a pastrycook's; the door was open, and the mistress herself behind the counter. There could be no harm in trying. But this time it was a determined refusal. Still, nothing was lost even where nothing was gained. She came back to her mamma, who was waiting while her bill was being made out. Mr. Chilton himself had come forward to speak to Mrs. Murray. He bowed to Bruey, and set a chair for her, drawing back while she eagerly showed her card. "Another sixpence, Mamma! It is getting on beautifully! But at the next shop they would not give anything, not even threepence, and I was *so* disappointed. Can you think of any one else I could ask while you are here?"

"I am only waiting for the bill, so there is no more time now."

Bruey's face looked an inch longer. Mr. Chilton stepped forward, and it shortened again.

"Will Miss Murray allow me to see her card?" he said, with the greatest politeness. He heard her speak of sixpences and threepences, and even if the object were not a particularly interesting one, he had no objection to gratify a customer to that small extent. He was rather magnificent in his personal appearance; and especially as her mamma was present, Bruey did not venture any appeal or explanation in this case, but gave him her card, with a bright and not altogether uneloquent smile.

"If Miss Murray would accept such a small contribution as one shilling, I should be most happy," he said.

Miss Murray was "most happy" to receive it, whatever Mr. Chilton might feel in giving it, and she was more than ever glad she had come out shopping with her mamma.

One or two more sixpences had been picked up by the time they reached Miss Benson's, and another before they left her.

The sun was very powerful as they returned up the hill, and Bruey flagged a little. She was not sorry to find that the lessons would have to be shortened. She had not much more than another week of lessons, for on Wednesday week Percy's holidays began, and hers were to begin at the same time, and the day before was his birthday, which would be at least a half-holiday to her. After that, there was some prospect of going to the seaside. The only drawback was, that she would not see Percy again till the beginning of August.

After her French and geography, "writing" stood next on the Thursday morning list. She took out her copybook, but did not begin. "Mamma, if I wrote it very nicely, would it not do as well as a copy if I wrote to Uncle Joseph this morning?"

"You might do that, if you won't keep asking me what to say."

"I know what I want to say, Mamma; so I will only ask you, if I am not sure how to spell a word."

By dinner-time the following note was ready:—

"8 Calton Terrace,
Thursday.

"Dearest Uncle Joseph,—I send you a collecting card which I am trying to fill for the Irish Society. Mamma says she will post you a newspaper, which will tell you some interesting things about it. We heard Mr. Brallaghan speak, and I think every one who heard him must have wished to do something for it. Please to read the 'Facts' on the cover of the card. And if you would send me a few stamps, I should be so much obliged. Percy was so good, he collected for me from some of his schoolfellows. He sends his love, and so does Mamma, and so does your very affectionate niece,

Bruey.

"*P.S.*—Please give my love to Aunt Joseph, and to Jessie, and Allan and Mary. Perhaps they would send me two stamps apiece; please ask them."

"Now, Mamma, if you would give me a good-sized envelope, my card can go with the letter. I shall copy the names on to my new card before tea, but I think I will send the old one to Uncle Joseph, because they will see Percy's hand on it."

After tea that evening, she called again at Mr. and Mrs. Smith's who had been out when she first went, and then at No. 13 and No. 15, No. 14 being empty. At No. 15 it was again "Not at home," so she left her card and a paper, saying she would call next day, and then went to play with Percy in the garden till suppertime. He was performing gymnastics in a large and spreading tree which they always declared grew on purpose. "Look out, Bruey! I'm going to swing off that bough." And he did it in a very agile fashion. "You couldn't do that!"

"I think I could! I should not mind trying." And she began to climb into the tree by some low boughs which made it pretty easy.

Mrs. Murray was trimming some roses, and looked up. "Bruey, what are you thinking of? what a state you will be in! You will ruin that frock. Come down; I can't allow you to be such a tomboy."

"Just this once, Mamma. It is so nice!"

"I daresay, but it will not be nice for me to have your frock all spoilt."

"I forgot my frock!" said Bruey, woefully, as she sprang to the ground. "I have not greened it at all yet, though, Mamma."

"That is a good thing. Now mind, Bruey, I will not have any climbing except on Saturday, when you have a cotton frock on that will have to go to the wash on Monday. And after the holidays I should think you will see that you are getting too old for it. Can't you have a game of croquet?"

"Oh! do, Percy; there will be just nice time for a four-ball game. Then I shall not be tantalised, Mamma, by seeing him up in the tree."

By that day-week the card had not only come back from Uncle Joseph's, with four names upon it—sum total enclosed 2s. 6d.—but it had made a journey to London and back to a dear godmother, and a whole half-crown in stamps came with the one name.

On the Sunday afternoon Bruey had sacrificed Miss Elizabeth Allison to the Irish Society, and had contrived to overtake and walk up with Miss Anstey instead, thereby securing, without much difficulty, a promise of sixpence, or maybe a shilling, if she liked to call for it next day.

So now, when Thursday morning's post brought the godmother's half-crown, the whole card was full. Actually thirty names! Her first visions had never reached more than half that number. They were made up thus—

Their own household	.5 names
The first morning's work in Calton Terrace. . . .	.6 "
Percy's schoolfellows	.4 "
Shops and dressmaker	.6 "
Further efforts in Calton Terrace	.3 "
Uncle and Cousins	.4 "
Godmother	.1 "
Miss Anstey	.1 "
Total	30 names

And yet there were further possibilities in more than one direction.

Never was her hat put on with greater pleasure than when, lessons being over, she was to go to No. 16 with the results of ten days' work. And if anything could have made her happier still, it was poor Miss Allison's warmly-expressed surprise and pleasure as she read the list of names and initials.

"I did not expect any one would get so many names as this, even if they might perhaps bring me more money. So I think I shall like your card best of all, because there is the most work in it. Was it very hard work, dear Bruey?"

"Sometimes. It is not nice asking, but when you get something it makes up for it."

"And even if one gets nothing, is there not something to make up for it?"

Bruey understood quite well that strong promise which came so sweetly into her mind on the hot morning when she had tried three houses running and got nothing had made up for it. And the happiness of the thought, *For Him!* and of the thanksgiving and prayer which grew out of it, had been more than enough to make up for a dozen flat refusals. She met Miss Allison's questioning look with such a light in her own brown eyes that the soft, shy "Yes!" conveyed a great deal of meaning. She had not seen enough of Miss Allison as yet to venture on any fuller answer in words.

"But you seem to have had famous experience of success; it is not every one who gets on so well. I don't wonder at your looking so bright this morning! Bruey, shall I tell you what your face made me think?"

A smile said mutely, "Please do!"

"I was thinking how kind it is of our good Master to give us so much *present* reward. Perhaps He gives this especially to His young workers, and it does seem such loving-kindness that He should so order it. Quite over and above the great joy of trying to please Him, and knowing that His smile is upon us and our work there is so much pleasure to be found in the work itself. And I think He means us to take this as His very kind and gracious 'present reward.' For instance, did you not enjoy the school treat very much more this year than when you only went to look on as a little visitor?"

"Oh, that I did! It was quite a different thing from standing about and feeling in the way, and getting hot and tired for nothing. I did not care to go again."

"What? not this year?"

"Oh dear, no, I mean last year. This time it was quite a different thing. I don't think I ever enjoyed anything so much, and I counted the days to it for a month before."

"Exactly; and every Sunday is full of interest to you now. And, ever since the Irish meeting, I think I am safe in guessing that you have enjoyed yourself very much on the whole?"

"Yes, that I have. Every one of the names on my card was a separate little piece of pleasure, which I should not have had without it."

"Well now, did you think of all that pleasure as given to you by the Master whom you are trying to serve? Did you say, '*Thou* hast put gladness in my heart'?"

"No, Miss Allison," said Bruey, thoughtfully, "I thought"——

"What did you think?"

"I don't know how to put it into words. But I thought that if I were very good indeed, I should not care so much about filling my card, and be so pleased at every fresh name."

"I see what you mean. You would like to do it *only* for Jesus Christ's sake. But I think you do. Suppose the Irish Society had been merely to teach the people to read the newspapers, would you have taken the trouble to ask for a single sixpence? Would you have cared in the least about it?"

She laughed. "No, certainly not!"

"Then you see, down at the bottom, you do wish to help our Master's cause, and do it for His sake. And I think we ought to be very thankful to Him when He gives us so much pleasure in doing it. I think it would make all our work happier still if we took not only every little bit of success, but every little feeling of pleasure and glee which arises out of it, as kindly sent from Him on purpose to make it easier and pleasanter to us. But now, what about the card? It need not have been sent in till the next first of March, and that is more than eight months to come. Would you not like to have another to keep by you, in case you come across any other generous persons?"

"That is what I came for! I have thought of some more 'Irish possibilities,' as my cousin calls them. I should like to get forty names. If we go to the seaside, I might meet some one whom I could ask. Last summer we went to Llandudno, and I made friends with nearly a dozen little boys and girls on the beach. I had no card then, but I daresay most of them would have given me sixpences if I had; or their mammas would."

"That is a good idea, and I wish it success. It is a hint for me, Bruey, for my doctor will perhaps allow me to go to the seaside, and I might make friends on the beach too!"

"I must not tire you, dear Miss Allison," said Bruey, as she rose to go, and kissed the gentle face of the invalid. "Please give my love to Miss Elizabeth."

"She will be pleased to hear of your success, but she is gone out this morning for a few days. So you came at a very good time, dear; for I am all alone, and it has been quite a pleasure."

Bruey could not have been expected to endure an empty card very long. By hook or by crook, at least a name or two to begin it must be obtained.

Cook brought in the tea that evening instead of the housemaid.

"Where is Jane?" asked Mrs. Murray.

"She bid me ask you to please to excuse her, ma'am, she does not feel well; I made her go and lie down, and took her a cup of tea."

"I will come and see her after tea. I noticed that she was very pale at dinner-time. Stay, I had better go at once."

She went, and when she came down again, Bruey asked if Jane was *very* poorly.

"No, I don't think there is much the matter. At least, nothing fresh. But she has been ailing so long that I see my only chance of keeping her is to let her have a long holiday at her home. That might set her up. She shall go as soon as Percy goes away, and then we can do for a few days, if Mrs. Fayling can come."

"And then, Mamma?"

"Then—we shall see!"

"But *what* shall we see, Mamma?"

"How can I tell?"

"Shall we see the sea, Mamma?" she said, kissing her. "Do say, yes!"

Mrs. Murray returned the kiss and added another, though she was not often demonstrative.

"I do not much like saying 'Yes' too positively, dear, but I am thinking about it. So you must be satisfied with, 'we shall see.' You often say that is nearly as good as 'Yes.'"

"Only not quite, Mamma, because it is not a promise."

"Ah, Bruey, promises are not worth much from human lips, however sincere. How do I know that I *could* fulfil this? No promises are sure but *His!*"

Bruey only answered by another kiss. What made her mother speak so solemnly? She clung lovingly to her for a minute, but then Percy burst in, and that always changed the subject.

After tea she opened another.

"Mamma, I have a grand scheme for this evening. May I go across to those large houses on the other side of the road along the top of Westwell Hill? It is not far, and I am sure Percy would come across with me if you would rather I did not go alone, and I should not very much mind trying. I need not go in, you know; I could send my card in and wait. I should think I should get a great deal there. Every one has a nice drive up to the door, and they have carriages and pairs."

Mrs. Murray laughed.

"If you are prepared to come back without a halfpenny you may go, but you had better not expect much there. Except Writton House, I should not wonder if Mrs. Courthope gave you a shilling. And mind you don't go to the last house; The Oaks, I think it is; they are Roman Catholics there."

Not a very lively prospect, but she would try. Percy escorted her to the gates of Alderley Lodge, and then left her, as she assured him she should not mind going alone, and it would be so stupid for him to wait at every door. The footman informed her that the family were gone out driving, and would return to dinner at half-past seven. Being "out" was not a refusal, and not to be ranked among failures. She would call again.

As she walked up the pretty drive of Carisbrooke House, she caught sight of delicate light dresses through the shrubs, and heard the sound of croquet mallets from the lawn on the other side of the house. She wished people would not have croquet parties just when she went collecting.

"Will you kindly show this to Mrs. or Miss Ayre?" she said to the man who opened the door. She wished she had not come to this house, for there was something very disagreeable and sarcastic in the bland way in which the tall fellow assured her the ladies were engaged with company, and could not be intruded upon.

"Thank you. It is of no consequence," she said, with all the little dignity she could command, and yet so gently and gravely that the footman felt the little lady had the best of it.

At Westwell House the footman was courteous enough, and took in her card as graciously as if it had been the visiting card of a carriage and pair. Still she wished people did not have footmen, and was very glad her mamma did not keep one. Calton Terrace might be less magnificent, but it had its advantages as a place of residence, and the absence of footmen was one. No, she would not care to live on Westwell Hill.

However, though the footman was personally unobjectionable, and politely sorry to return her the card without any answer, that did not remove the impression against Westwell Hill. For those who lived in grand houses like these *could* give if they liked. And if they did not like, so much the worse for them.

It was relieving that Writton House came next, but damping to hear that Mrs. Courthope was out; and again came the temptation to give it up, and not go to the next house. She stood undecided for a minute, and then asked the servant to tell her who lived at The Quarry, next door. "It is the residence of Mrs. Fitzgerald," he replied; adding spitefully, "She is an invalid, I believe, and never sees strangers," with a tone which implied, "so it is no earthly use *your* going!" For the card in Bruey's hand, and the question about next door, made him feel sure she was a collector—a race of beings to which he objected on principle, as causing unnecessary wear and tear to the door-bells, and as being some degrees worse than common beggars, because they had not the excuse of personal poverty, and must therefore be, one and all, impudent impostors. He might learn better when he had been longer at Writton House, but at present he was new to it, an importation from a London square.

That minute's delay issued in good. At the gate she met Mr. and Mrs. Courthope themselves. Half a minute sooner or later, and she would have missed them. She was not quite certain who it was, but they kindly noticed her embarrassment, and set her at ease by a courteous question as to her errand, and, on hearing it, asked her to come in with them.

The result of a little delicate inquiry, so well managed as to bring out who she was, and where she came from, and how she came to be a collector, without any apparent curiosity, was that Mr. Courthope said softly to his wife, "My dear,

I think we may as well do what we were speaking of; what do you think?" and the answer was, "Yes, I see no objection; and perhaps it will be a stimulus, and so be more useful than if sent direct."

Thereupon Mr. Courthope addressed Bruey, who was quite mystified as to what could be coming, and told her that he and Mrs. Courthope had been at the Irish meeting, and had felt inclined to become subscribers. That no one had called for any subscriptions; and that though they had thought of sending a contribution to the Society's house in Dublin, yet, among so many other calls, it would, perhaps, have been forgotten. But as a little collector had called, they would be glad to make her the channel of the little subscription. And a sovereign and a shilling were laid upon the table before Bruey's astonished eyes. A guinea for her card! Was it possible?

Mr. Courthope himself accompanied her to the door, and spoke so kindly about her little work, that she ventured to ask him (the footman not being in sight), whether he thought it would be any use calling at Mrs. Fitzgerald's. "By all means," he answered; "not that I can assure you of success, but I hope you will try, for her sake. Do not send your card in, or you will have nothing, but ask to see her."

He went back to his wife.

"What a nice simple child that is," she said. "There is a singular tone of reality about her."

"Yes," he answered, "I think her heart is in it, though I like her none the less for being shy and modest about it. One is thankful to see young workers rising up, but there is room for many more. That child's simple energy and determination will be worth a great deal when she grows up."

"How frightened she looked when we met her! As if she were caught trespassing. You have sent her 'on her way rejoicing' now. An unexpected contribution is worth more than itself; it is a great impetus."

Bruey was shown into Mrs. Fitzgerald's drawing-room, where the old lady sat in state with closed windows, though the air was still and even oppressively warm without. She recollected Mrs. Madingley's sixteenpenny Valenciennes, which had seemed an obstacle to charity, and wondered whether the magnificent lappets of Mrs. Fitzgerald's cap, which must have cost something alarming, would stand in the way also.

"My dear, you must excuse me," was the encouraging reply when Bruey had told her Irish story. "People think I am made of money. And they don't know!" shaking her head at the words, as if the workhouse were likely to be her next step in life, by way of enlightening, once for all, the people who were in such sad ignorance of her position. "My dear, they don't know!" she repeated. "Rates and taxes, and water and gas, and police and poor-rates, my dear, you can't imagine! Even my poor Lily to be paid for! And my granddaughters expecting jewellery from grandmamma, and one of them going to be married to the nephew of Lord Arklow; you could see it in the peerage, my dear, a branch of the Meath family; and wedding present from Howell and James, my dear; they don't know what one is obliged to do in these days, and everything double the price since the railways and telegraphs, and my maid asking for more wages. All, my dear, young people don't know how one's little bit of money goes."

Had Bruey been deaf, she would have judged by Mrs. Fitzgerald's countenance that her lips were detailing some harrowing tale of woe and calamity. In vain she tried to move the old lady's pity with a further representation of the spiritual needs of the poor Irish.

"My dear, the Irish always were beggars, and always will be. And if you had them taught to read, they would only write begging letters. And, my dear, you couldn't believe it, but I have had begging letters from far and near, till I should be ruined—ruined, my dear, if I did not put them in the fire. Don't you ever write begging letters, my dear. Nobody ever attends to them."

It was hopeless altogether, so Bruey rose. The old lady touched a bell at her side, and said, "Good-bye, my dear; I hope you will not take cold going out into the air with your thin frock. Young people don't think."

At that instant a maid opened the door, behind which the old lady's armchair was placed, while Bruey stood with her back to it. She started and gave a little scream, for a good-sized white dog bounced upon her without any warning, and as the assault was from behind, she could not see whether it was in play or in earnest—in fact, did not see the dog at all, till its sudden irruption nearly knocked her down. So, though not at all afraid of dogs in general, it was no wonder that she was startled and frightened.

"Lily, pretty darling! Naughty Lily, come to her mistress then! Poor Lily!" cried Mrs. Fitzgerald.

"Down, Lily!" said the maid who had opened the door; "ha' done then! She will not hurt you, Miss; it's only her play."

Bruey tried to be calm, though she could not help trembling. Lily bounced away to her mistress, and then the maid discovered a terrible tear in Bruey's pretty muslin frock. "Nasty dog!" she said, relieving her mind by saying the words very softly, seeing that her mistress was too much occupied with Lily's rough gambols to overhear. "Dear, dear, dear! see how she has torn your frock, Miss. If you will allow me, I'll pin it together to do till you get home."

The maid stooped low to examine the damage more closely, but looked up hastily as she felt Bruey's hand heavily on her shoulder, and saw something was wrong. Bruey felt very queer; her heart began to thump violently, and she thought she must have fallen down, but that the maid quickly supported her, and put her on the nearest sofa. She closed her eyes, and felt too ill, though relieved by lying down, to notice much of what passed for the next few minutes.

"Gracious me! She isn't dying? Ring the bell, Horton, for the carriage to take her home. Down, Lily dear! To think of this! Has she fainted, Horton? Where is my smelling-bottle? Oh dear, oh dear, Horton! don't you see how upset I am? Poor Lily, down then! What is it, Horton? I am sure Lily would not bite."

Horton rang the bell and found a smelling-bottle for the old lady, and another for Bruey in a moment.

"It's only—I don't know—my heart beats so," said she, closing her eyes again.

"Don't speak, my dear," said Horton, kindly; "please to lie still."

Poor Bruey could not have done anything else at that moment, but she was glad of the kind tone.

"It's palpitations, Ma'am, from the fright; don't put yourself about, she will be better presently. Bring a glass of water, John," she added, as the footman answered the bell.

Horton remained beside her, kindly hushing her when she attempted to move or speak, and doing what in her lay towards calming her mistress's perturbation. In a little while the palpitation grew less, and after a long quarter of an hour the little heart was tolerably quiet, though the pulse still fluttered.

"Thank you; I'm so much better, I can go home now."

"Wait a little longer," said Horton, who was rather captivated by the touching little smile which accompanied Bruey's words.

"Hadn't you better let her go, if she is able?" suggested Mrs. Fitzgerald. "She might be taken worse again, and then what in the world should I do? One never knows—ah, people don't know!"

"She is coming round nicely, Ma'am; but it might bring it on again if she got up in a hurry. Is it far to where you live, Miss?"

"Oh no; only Calton Terrace, not five minutes' walk," she answered.

"John can see her home," said Mrs. Fitzgerald.

"Oh please not!" said Bruey. Then recollecting herself, she said, "You are very kind, but I can go by myself quite well, thank you."

"It is a very little way," said Horton; "perhaps if you could spare me that long, Ma'am, I had better see her across myself."

"It is very inconsiderate of you, Horton, when you see how upset I am. And Miss Murray says she can go by herself."

Horton made no reply, but said, "Excuse me, Ma'am; I shall be back in a minute."

"Do you feel better, my dear? Are you subject to these attacks? Palpitation is always so alarming to those who are not used to you."

Bruey did not feel inclined to talk, she merely replied, "Better, thank you."

In a few minutes Horton returned. "If Miss Murray thinks she can walk, Eliza will be pleased to go across with her." Bruey was able to walk, though she felt very trembling still; but she would be so glad to get home, that she did not wish to stay longer on Mrs. Fitzgerald's sofa than was necessary.

"Good-bye, my dear; I hope you will be in stronger health soon. You must not be frightened at Lily. Poor Lily! she has gone to sleep after it all. Good-bye; I hope you won't take cold."

Horton took her downstairs, and made her sit down in the dining-room for a few minutes, insisting on her drinking half a cup of tea, and eating a biscuit before setting out on the home-journey, committing her then to the care of Eliza, a good-tempered young housemaid, whose sympathies Horton had enlisted on Bruey's behalf during her short absence from the drawing-room.

Bruey warmly thanked Horton for her kindness, and with Eliza's ready arm, and slow walking, with occasional pauses, she reached No. 8 safely.

Her mother had been expecting her for some time, but it was not late enough to cause anxiety. She was far more distressed than she allowed Bruey to see, when she heard what had passed. She hoped the delicacy and weakness about the heart were being outgrown, and though there was nothing dangerous in such an attack in itself, it was an indication that care and watchfulness were still needed; and the mother's heart was very heavy when she had seen her Bruey safe into bed, and sat down by the window in the twilight to think it over.

As for Bruey herself, she was so supremely happy in her guinea, that she thought little, in comparison, of her less pleasant experiences at The Quarry, and it was not till next morning that she found she had forgotten her card.

As for the difficult problem of repairing the effects of Lily's "play," so that the muslin should be fit to appear in, that did not trouble poor Mrs. Murray at all. It was rather a relief than otherwise to have to do it—*for Bruey*.

CHAPTER XII.

CHANGE OF WEATHER.

BRUEY did not feel very mighty when she woke next morning, and was not sorry to be condemned to breakfast in bed; but in the course of the day she felt quite well again. Her mamma had some very opportune business in the town, which made an excellent excuse for excusing the lessons.

Towards evening a footman came with " Mrs. Fitzgerald's compliments, and to inquire how the young lady was," leaving an envelope addressed to Miss Murray, which " required no answer." It contained the forgotten card, which Percy had volunteered to go and fetch before night, and three shillings and a note.

"THE QUARRY, *Friday Evening.*

" Sarah Horton begs to return the collecting card left by Miss Murray last evening, and hopes Miss Murray will accept a small contribution from the servants at The Quarry. S. H. was very sorry Miss Murray should have been put about by the dog, and all hope Miss Murray has recovered from the effects of it."

Who would have thought of this! Now that it was all over, Bruey thought she would not mind either dogs or palpitations if such results followed.

Saturday morning was hotter than ever. The heat of the last few days had been unusual for this side Midsummer Day.

Soon after twelve o'clock Percy appeared. " I tell you what, it's no trifle to walk up out of Rilverton in this broil. You look enviably cool."

" Come and rest in the shade, then. You are in good time to-day."

" Well, it was no fun staying; the playground was like an oven, and the streets would not be any cooler for waiting, and the sooner one was under a green tree the better. So I came straight, and now I can cool myself."

Grown-up persons commonly sit still for that purpose; boys have other modes. Percy's consisted in a leisurely rolling and kicking on the grass in his shirt sleeves. This performance was supposed to rest him, and cool him, and soothe him, and do him good generally. After a prolonged course of this home-made prescription, he started up and surveyed the boughs overhead in a business-like way.

"Let's have a climb! Aunt gave you leave for Saturday mornings, and that's the frock that goes into the tub on Monday, isn't it? See what a good boy I am to remember the conditions!"

Bruey jumped up. There was nothing to hinder, certainly, and the great green house above them was no hotter than the green floor below. So up the two went, climbing and creeping from bough to bough, at no very great height to be sure, but just enough to make it interesting and desirable not to slip.

"Now I'm going to swing off that bough again! Look out, Bruey! Here goes!" And he swung off in style.

But the "look out" was just too late, for Bruey was at that moment performing a critical passage from one bough to another, and the sudden shake of Percy's "swing off" dislodged her firmest foot, while she had no decided hold for the other, and would have fallen from a sufficient height to have endangered her bones, but for the sudden and firm grasp which she managed to get upon a small branch at the very instant of the slip. But her feet dangled in the air, and sought vainly for a footing, while her whole weight hung upon the small branch by her hands.

She cried out to Percy. He lost no time in coming to the rescue, but his "swing off" had taken him far out of reach. He had to spring to the ground, run to the other side of the tree, and climb up by the way they first mounted in order to reach her.

"Hold tight, Bruey! I'm coming! Don't let go!" he cried.

"Make haste, Percy! I can't hold much longer," she cried. She must drop if he could not reach her quickly, for her hands could not bear the strain any longer, and she must be hurt if she dropped, for it was a long way to the ground. There was an unheard cry, as well as that which reached Percy's ear, "Oh save me, keep me from falling!" And as that cry went up through the green roof and beyond the blue dome, she felt Percy's hand seize her foot, and place it on a bough which she had felt for, but could not find. That was enough; she was safe, for it relieved the strain on her wrists, and a second footing was then easily found. In a few minutes she was standing at the foot of the tree, looking up at the place where she had so narrowly escaped a bad fall.

"That came of your having good wrists; some girls couldn't have caught and held on like that." Did it? She felt it came of Him who gave strength to her wrists, and presence of mind to grasp the branch, and endurance to hold on till Percy reached her. She did not speak, but sat down, and in a minute or so lay down on the grass. "Bruey, what's the matter? You are not hurt? I say; what is it, Bruey?"

"Hush!—all right; stop!" and she caught his hand, lest he should run for her mamma. "Wait one minute!" He was frightened, for she panted and trembled, but she would not let him go, and smiled to reassure him. At last she got out, "Don't go—I shall be all right directly—only my heart beating—because I was frightened." He sat down by her, and waited till she had recovered herself. It was not such violent palpitation as on Thursday evening.

"I would rather you did not say anything about it," she said, when it had passed; "it would only vex Mamma for nothing, and it is quite gone now. She used to be so troubled about it when I was quite a little girl after I had fever, but I have not had it for ever so long till Thursday evening, and I saw it vexed her then a little. But indeed it does not matter; see, I am well now! It was so stupid of me to slip."

"No, it wasn't! It was I that was stupid, not to have looked to see that you were all square before I swung off."

They went in to dinner as if nothing had happened. Mrs. Murray seemed troubled. She told Jane not to wait when she had brought the dinner in, they would help themselves to the vegetables.

"Jane keeps so poorly," she said, "that I see it is no use going on. I must let her write to her mother today, and go on Monday; and I must get Mrs. Fayling to come and do her work."

Percy had a bathing engagement, and departed early in the afternoon, telling his aunt not to expect him till supper-time.

After tea Mrs. Murray said she should go down to see about Mrs. Fayling, and Bruey might come with her if she liked. "Shall you be going again at the beginning of the week, Mamma?"

"I don't know; I may or I may not. But do just as you feel inclined; it is very hot and oppressive, and if you would rather stay in the garden, do."

She thought it over. It could not be quite so hot coming back, and Percy would not be at home; and though she felt tired and dull, it must be more tiring and dull for poor Willie Fosbery in that dismal Gilling's Yard, and she knew her little visits were a great pleasure to him. There was the chance of Monday or Tuesday, to be sure, and she might be less tired then. But suppose mamma should not go, and suppose they went to the sea at the end of the week, this might be the last opportunity for no one knew how long. So she went.

Willie was in his little chair as usual, outside the door. It was the end house of the yard, so there were no passers-by, and very seldom anything to interrupt. Alice brought a chair out of the house for Miss Murray, and then went back to the Saturday evening cleaning-up, which her mother had set her to do. He passed his hand over his great forehead.

"It has been so hot all day. I wonder if it's cooler for the birds than for us. They have got more air, but then they fly up nearer the sun. If I was the birds, I would keep away from the bricks. There's one now atop of that chimney!"

"It did not stay, though," said Bruey; "it has flown away. But perhaps some of them do go out of town in summer, and only come back in the winter, because they can find more to eat."

"I wish I was one of them," sighed Willie. "When you brought me the blue-bells last month, I used to shut my eyes and fancy I was a sparrow flying through the air over the chimney-pots, and then away to where the bluebells grew. And I fancied it over and over again, till one night I dreamt it, and it was all like real, and it came so cool to my head under the trees; and then I woke, and found Alice had got up, and put the window open because it was morning."

Bruey thought of her mother's pleasant little garden, and the green tree under which she could sit any day. The only green Willie could see was a dusty geranium or two in the dirty windows. Even weeds did not grow in Gilling's Yard.

"When were you last in the country, Willie?"

"Three summers ago. Uncle was alive then; and Mr. Irby, where he used to live, sent his carriage for him and me too, and we went to Holmwood Park, and I sat on the grass all the afternoon under big trees, like a beautiful street, only trees instead of homes. We should have gone the next summer, but poor uncle died. I used to wonder whether heaven was more like that, because it was so beautiful; and when the sun got lower, it turned more like gold than green. And it says gold streets, you know."

Bruey did not take up the thread of Willie's fancies, because her busy little brain had begun to scheme some way of getting Willie into the country for a day. What a pleasure that would be! She was silent, so Willie began again. He was far more communicative than he had been three months ago.

"Miss Bruey, I've got ninepence-halfpenny on my card, and there's three-pence more promised. There's summer and autumn and winter to come before the first of March, and I shall get more by then, for they comes and goes—comes and goes."

He meant the population of Gilling's Yard, where he himself was quite an old inhabitant.

"I think that is a great deal, Willie; you must have asked a great many people to get all that, for I daresay some said 'No.'"

"Well, not many did; they mostly had a halfpenny."

"Perhaps I shall not see you again for a long time, Willie; I can't tell, but I may be going away very soon."

"Going away, Miss Bruey?"

"Don't look so sorry, Willie. I only wish you could go too. It won't be for very long, and then I shall see you again."

But Willie did look sorry. Bruey's visits had made all the difference to his gloomy little life; and what should he do without her, even for a little while?

"It won't be for very long?" he repeated.

"No. Besides, I do not know for certain yet, and perhaps I shall see you again before I go, so I shall not say good-bye this evening; only, Willie, in case I should not see you again, I should like to leave you a good-bye text for you to keep in your heart all the while I am away. Shall I?"

"Yes, please. I recollect your texts better than any others."

"It is a text that came into my mind one day when I was collecting, and I always like to give you the texts that God seems to have given to me. It is— '*As I was with Moses, so will I be with thee.*' Mamma helped me to find it, and it comes twice over, in the 1st and in the 3rd of Joshua. I was thinking that, as we have nearly finished Genesis, it would be nice to go on with Exodus (that begins the story of Moses, you know), and then read Numbers, and all the way through we might recollect this text, and keep putting little marks against every verse that shows us how the Lord was with Moses, and then we could always remember, '*So I will be with thee.*'"

"But God couldn't be with us like He was with Moses. Moses was such a great man."

"Don't you know God says, '*Moses, my servant*'? But He has some great servants, and some little servants; and if you and I are His little servants, I think He will be with us just as much as if we were great servants. At least, I don't *think* it, I *know* it, because there the words are! And besides, Willie," she added, softly, "*it comes true;* I feel it sometimes as if He really did help me, and be with me."

Mrs. Murray came out of Mrs. Fayling's door, and this put an end to the talk, for she came and asked Willie if his mother was in.

"She is gone marketing, Ma'am, with Hetty, but Alice is in."

Alice heard her name, and came out.

"Alice," said Mrs. Murray, "I wanted Mrs. Fayling to come up on Monday for a few days, but she is engaged, and cannot tell me of any one else. She tells me you are fairly handy. Could I depend on you to be steady and industrious if I try to manage with you instead?"

Alice was ready with any amount of promises. It was just what she would like, to go for a few days to a place, and not feel tied down for a long time to hard work. She had had a taste of that at her nursemaid's place. And she had heard Mrs. Fayling speak warmly of Mrs. Murray, while Miss Bruey was privately an object of great attraction, though she did not know why.

"Very well, then; you must be up at Calton Terrace about half-past six on Monday morning, and you had better bring what little things you may want for four or five days, as it will be more convenient for you to stay altogether than to go home at night."

How wistful Willie's eyes were!

"Good evening, Willie," said Mrs. Murray. "Bruey, we must not delay; do you see how suddenly it has clouded over? I think we shall have tempest before night."

"Good-bye, Willie!" said Bruey. "There is a storm coming, and we must make haste home."

The tall houses of Gilling's Yard had hidden the rapidly rising clouds; but as Mrs. Murray and Bruey came out into the open street, they saw a heavy thunder-cloud coming up grandly from the east, and a low rumble, not to be mistaken for wheels, announced the coming tempest.

"How nice and cool it will be for school and church to-morrow, Mamma," said Bruey, "if we have a good storm to-night."

"Yes, dear; but I hope it will not come just yet. I am positively obliged to call at Mrs. George's, but I think I would rather you went on home without waiting for me. You don't mind?"

"Oh, no! Mamma, I should like it better, for I am very tired. But do try and get home yourself before the storm comes."

They separated, and Bruey walked slowly on alone. Like great black wings the thunder-cloud mounted the sky, while the rumble grew into peals, and just as Bruey reached the foot of the Westwell Hill, on the side of which Calton Terrace stood, a vivid flash cleft the grim curtain, and a crash right overhead, like a great explosion, made her start and run. She did not mind thunder and lightning when in-doors, but who would care to be out longer than they could help in such a storm as had begun? As if the flash and the peal had burst open the gates of "the waters that were above the firmament," without even the usual warning of large, slow drops, down came a shower enough to prove the vanity of any so-called waterproofs. But she had none. Though every one expected it, after such sultry weather, no one expected it quite so soon. In a few minutes Bruey's frock was clinging round her like a wet sheet. She was obliged to stop running, for a few rapid steps made her heart begin to beat, and what should she do if violent palpitation came on, though it was hardly five minutes' walk farther? It was no use waiting, for she had passed the last shelter just as the storm burst, and there was nothing for it but to go on, getting soaked to the skin, and not daring to quicken her pace, lest the beating should increase.

Oh how glad she was to reach No. 8! No one heard her come in, and she threw herself down, all wet as she was, on the dining-room sofa. Anything to quiet the palpitation, which was so distressing. She would get up and ring the bell when that was better. How long she lay she did not know; it seemed like half-an-hour. Probably it was ten minutes. But that was long enough for mischief.

At last Jane's step was heard in the hall, and she called out.

"Why, Miss Bruey, I never heard you come in! Dear me, Miss, what a state you are in!"

And Bruey, who was beginning to feel the chill and discomfort of her wet clothes, as the palpitation went off, was very thankful to get upstairs, and have Jane's help in taking them off. She shivered.

"You are quite chilled, Miss, lying on the sofa in those wet things. If I were you, I would get into bed at once, and I will bring you a cup of tea. When will your mamma be back?"

"I should think she will wait at Mrs. George's till the storm is over, or ride up. Oh dear, I hope she won't get wet! Thank you, Jane, I should like to lie down, but I don't want any tea, thank you."

"You had better have it, Miss, to take the chill off; it won't take two minutes to make."

"No, never mind, thank you." And she lay down.

Jane went downstairs, and reported matters to the cook, who agreed with her that it was right and proper Miss Bruey should have something warm at once.

"O Jane, how naughty of you, when you are so poorly, to go fetching me tea upstairs!"

"There, Miss Bruey, we thought it was not that you could not drink it! I feel better this evening, and if I didn't, I wasn't likely to see you catch your death of cold, and not bring you anything."

The warm tea was very comfortable.

"It was very kind of you to bring it, Jane."

"It isn't many things more I can do for you, Miss Bruey," said she, beginning to cry. "I am going away on Monday, and there's no knowing whether Missis will ever have me back again. I've been in a poor way this long time, and

I know I'm not fit for service. It has been very good of your mamma to keep me as she has."

"Poor dear Jane!" said Bruey, taking her hand kindly.

"It was always a pleasure to wait on you, Miss Bruey. It is a great trial to have to go away and be a burden to my parents."

Bruey raised herself a little, and said, "I can't tell what it feels like, because I never had to leave a place and be a burden; but I am very sorry for you. And I wish I could comfort you."

Jane cried, and Bruey looked at her sympathisingly. A bright thought struck her, and she said, "Jane, please go into the dressing-room, and in the corner of the table-drawer you will find a little text-book. Please bring it here."

It was brought, and Bruey turned it over till she found two texts which seemed to suit her thought. She turned down a leaf at each place, and put the book into Jane's hand, saying, "Look at the places where I have turned the leaves down, and then perhaps you will not be quite so sad. And take the little book home with you; I can do without it. And will you promise me something, to please me?"

She would promise anything that was possible.

"Will you read the text for the day out of it, every day till you see me again?"

The promise was given. Who knows what fruit it bore!

Just then Mrs. Murray came in. She had not been anxious about Bruey, as she calculated that she would have reached home before the storm began, and had not allowed for the slower pace of more than usually tired feet. When she heard the whole story, she could not help a troubled feeling about her child; palpitations again, and a chill,—how could she tell whether illness might not follow? Though Bruey smilingly assured her that she was "quite warm now, Mamma, and so comfortable," she lay awake much that night, often placing her ear near to the heart of the dear little sleeper, that she might be sure there was no fluttering.

CHAPTER XIII.

PERCY'S EXPLANATION.

SUNDAY morning was chilly and unsettled. The storm had passed, but had left discontented fragments of cloud, which might gather in strong force any hour, and the fine settled weather of the last three weeks was evidently at an end for the present.

Bruey's morning sleep was late and heavy. It was close upon breakfast-time when she started up, and saw her mother dressed, and bending over her Bible.

"O Mamma, I shall be late!"

Mrs. Murray rose and came to her, hushing her down again. "No, it is not late for you."

It was some minutes before the sleep was fairly thrown off, and then she was eager to get up.

"I am not ill, dear Mamma; do let me. I shall be late for school, indeed."

"Dear pet, you are not going to school this morning; you will lie still a little while, and have your breakfast. The bell is just going to ring, and you would not be in time, so just lie still."

"O Mamma, I do wish you had woke me! I must go to school. Miss Allison won't be there, and I must go to my little girls."

"Bruey, dear child, hush and listen," said Mrs. Murray, speaking very quietly. "You are not very well, and if you started off this morning you might be very ill, and then think how it would trouble me! When God gave you work to do, you were glad to do it, but to-day He tells you to be still, and leave your work to others. You are not going to rebel against Him, Bruey?"

"No, Mamma; but there is no one to take my children, unless one of the big girls goes. And they won't like that!"

"Don't you think that He who sent you to those little children, is kind enough and able enough to take care of them, and have them taught without you?"

"I did not think of it that way, Mamma. And I thought I *ought* to go."

"But you are quite sure you ought to obey me. And I am quite sure I am right in saying you are not to go to-day. There is the bell."

After prayers Mrs. Murray came up again. Bruey was lying quiet and contented.

"Mamma, is Percy down?" she said.

"Yes, dear."

"Might I speak to him for one minute?"

"What is it? Cannot I tell him?"

"Yes, you *could,* but please let me speak to him myself. Only for a minute." Percy was called up.

"What's the mischief, Bruey? Got a cold? Your humble servant, Ma'am! Any orders this morning, Ma'am?"

But he soon saw that his cousin was not in a mood for nonsense, though she smiled cheerfully; and he toned down accordingly. There was something about her which quieted him that morning.

"I have a great request to make," she said, "will you grant it me?"

It was not like Percy to answer with a quiet and matter-of-fact "Yes, dear. What is it?" But he did.

"I should be so glad—oh! I can't tell you how glad—if you would go down to the school for me, and tell Miss Anstey, or whoever takes Miss Allison's place, that I am not coming to-day. And O Percy!"——She looked pleadingly at him and stopped.

"Well, what? I don't mind the run down there, I am sure. I shall be back in a quarter of an hour, and can report progress to you."

"Oh, if you only would—would you, Percy?—just this once, stop and teach my little girls instead of me? If you don't, they will only have one of the great girls sent to them, and I would so much rather you would teach them! I can't ask you another Sunday, you know."

This was rather too much for Percy's good-nature. *He* teach small girls? Not he! He would go collecting all down High Street first! Besides, what could he teach them? If it were the multiplication table, or *hic, hæc, hoc,* well and good, but they didn't want that, he supposed. He had no doubt Bruey talked to them like any parson, and he was sure he could do no such thing.

She stopped him. "Percy dear, if I told you exactly what I was going to teach them, I am sure you would not mind just doing that. See, this is the text," and she took a little paper out of her Bible, "and these are some of the questions I meant to ask them about it. But you would make better ones out of your own head, I know, as you went on. And these are the back texts which they must say over. And they know the first two verses of the 24th hymn, so they will have to learn the third verse to-day." She gave him no time to object, but went on. "And I was going to tell them about the Transfiguration, in the 17th of St. Matthew, and that is easy and beautiful to tell; you can't think how pleased they will be with that story; you'll see!"

"But I never said I was going to teach them! I said I couldn't!"

"Yes, you can, Percy, and you *will*. And you will like it so much when you have once begun."

Percy fidgeted and looked serious.

"Bruey, I really can't. Fact is, I'm not good enough,"

"I don't think anybody would do much if they waited till they felt good enough. Dear Per! If you will go, I will ask God to help you, and to make you like doing it, and to make you very glad that you went. And you will ask Him too, while you are walking down, won't you?"

She gained her little victory. But it was doubtful whether Percy would ever have consented, had it not been for this "something" about his little cousin which tamed him. It was harder to resist her when she was so poorly and gentle.

As he walked down, he looked to see what text Bruey had chosen. It was evidently meant to be connected with the Transfiguration story: "*Thine eyes shall see the King in His beauty; they shall behold the land that is very far off.*" He could imagine what she would have said about it, and how she would have tried to tell the little ones about the glorious beauty of the Lord Jesus, the King, whom having not seen, she certainly loved. No wonder if they listened, if she spoke it out of her very heart and through her very eyes, as she did to him on that always silently remembered Sunday evening! They would want to see Him, and feel inclined to love Him, if *she* told them about Him. But what had he to say about Him? What did he know and feel? Never in his life before had Percy felt so strongly that sense of ignorance which leads to blessed knowing, that sense of being very far off which leads to coming near.

Very humbly he went and sat in Bruey's place; and if his teaching that morning was not very brilliant, his learning was perhaps deeper than it had ever been.

For the next day or two, though "not ill," Bruey was certainly "not well." Lessons were not attempted. She looked at pictures a little, and read a little, but felt most inclined to lie on the sofa and do nothing. More than once she felt so unaccountably dismal, that she had a good cry when no one was by, all about nothing. And it was curiously difficult to answer amiably about things which need not have disturbed her temper in the least. Was all that old battle going to be fought over again? And she had another cry at the thought.

On Monday morning Alice came and Jane went.

She was the more pleased at Alice's coming, as it would pave the way for her plan about Willie. She unfolded this to her mamma. If Willie might come up the first fine day before they went away, she would attend to him, so that it need be no trouble to any one. "How was he to come?" She had planned that. Mrs. Madingley had a strong perambulator, constructed to carry two, or even three on emergency, and her babies did not go out till about half-past ten. She was sure Mrs. Madingley would lend the perambulator, if mamma would spare Alice to go with it for him at half-past nine. Then he could sit in the garden all day, till Alice had done her work in the evening, and Mrs. Madingley's babies were gone to bed, and then he could be taken home. It would be as much to him as the seaside trips would be to herself. Mrs. Murray's "We will see!" was in a tolerably encouraging tone.

Tuesday was Percy's birthday, but she did not see him before he went to school, and found he had left word that he should dine with one of the boys who lived close to the school, in order to save time, as some special breaking-up affair was going on. It was nearly sunset when he came back; it was cool and windy, and the evening light was pale and watery. There had been no time for thought before; but he could not forget that it was his fourteenth birthday, now that the bustling day, and the whole half-year too, were over. Fourteen! and Bruey was only twelve. But he felt as if she were older in some things. He wished he had not gone to the Sunday school, that text would keep haunting him so. Whose *"eyes"*? Bruey's, he was sure, would *"see the King in His beauty,"* but would *his*? Would it be beautiful to him if he did see the King? And if not, what then? He would not think about it; he was determined. Bother the Sunday school! Fourteen—fifteen—sixteen—twenty. So it would go on; where would it stop? It *would* stop, this life of days and years, which had run up to fourteen already. Bother his birthday! Why did people tell him when he was born, and keep count? It would stop all the same if they had not. And then? And *then?* What possessed him to mope like this? Why did the text come back as an almost mocking answer—*Then, "Thine eyes shall see the King"?* He wished he need never see Him, wished he had never heard the verse, wished he had never been born.

In this mood he reached the house. Bruey was lying on the sofa, covered over. It had seemed cold to her. He came in and kissed her. "Good morning!" he said, playfully. "I should not even have said 'Good-night' if I had been much later, by the look of it."

"No, I am going to bed soon; but it is not too late to wish you many happy returns. It has not seemed like a birthday; you have been away, and I have been so tired, so very tired, all day."

"Birthdays used to be jolly," said Percy, tilting his chair back. "Somehow it is a moping business now."

"Is it? Well, I don't know that. I think my last birthday was the nicest I ever had, and I wanted yours to be nice too. Do you know, while I have been lying here, watching the clouds, I was thinking about your birthday, and about the text you taught my children for me. It seems so nice for a birthday text, '*Thine eyes shall see the King in His beauty.*'"

Percy tilted his chair down with a bump that made her start. "That's odd! that *is* odd!" he said.

"Why odd?" she asked.

"Why, because that text bothered me all the way home, as if some one kept dinning it into my ears. And here you have been at it too!"

"It's beautiful, I think," said Bruey. "It is a promise, and God does not keep some of His promises, but all of them. So we *shall* 'see.'"

She said it musingly, and as if more to herself than to Percy. He had his back to the window, so that she could not see his face very well, though the evening light fell softly upon hers. There was again that "something" about her which had quieted him on Sunday morning. He fidgeted a little, and then said in a low voice, "But, Bruey, what if I don't want to see Him at all?" He thought a loving and pitying angel's face might have looked something like hers, as she said—

"Not want to see *Him,* Percy dear,—'*the King in His beauty*'? You would, if you loved Him."

"But I don't love Him, Bruey, and that's the fact; and I don't see how I am to, that's more. I would if I could."

"I know one can't of one's self. And yet it seems most extraordinary that one didn't *always* love Him, when one only thinks of His loving us so much as to die for us, and forgiving us everything. But one does not see it till He sends the Holy Spirit to make us see it and feel it. I can't explain it, but I know it is so. I have asked God every day, for a long time, to give me the Holy Spirit, that He may show me more of Jesus, and make me love Him more; and I want you to promise me something."

Percy came nearer.

"You are going away to-morrow, and I shall not see you again till August. Will you ask every day what I ask?"

"Tell it me again, then."

"That God would give you the Holy Spirit to show you '*His* beauty,' till you can't help loving Him, and to show you that you cannot do without Him too. Every day till I see you again! Will you, Per?"

He promised, and they were silent for a few minutes:

"Satan will try to hinder you from keeping on asking, Percy; but you have promised."

"That's very likely. He is up to that! Something always hinders one. And it is hardest to keep clear of just what hinders one most."

"*Let us lay aside every weight,*" said Bruey.

"I may as well make a clean breast of it," said Percy, with a great effort. "I believe I should have got ever so much better after that Sunday evening (you know when I mean), if it had not been for one thing."

He stopped.

"Don't tell me if you would rather not."

"No, I'd rather, now I've begun. The fellows lend me books—books I guess Aunt would not like, and that I can't leave about or read downstairs because of that, and they are so amusing and interesting that I always want to go on, and when I have finished one I want another. And then I read these after I came up to bed. I put the gas down very low when I heard Aunt coming up, and turned it up again when I heard her safe in her room. Sometimes I went on till after twelve o'clock, and then I bundled into bed without saying my prayers. Then I thought I would always say my prayers first, and then I could read as long as I liked without feeling I had *got* to say them; but that did not answer either, for it did not feel like saying prayers at all. I was right in the middle of a very interesting book that Sunday, and I did mean to have turned over a new leaf, but I could not resist going on with it next night, and then there seemed no help for it."

"Was it one of those yellow ones I saw in your drawer once?"

"Yes. I wish I had never read one of them, but if I had one to-night I don't believe I could help reading it."

"Did Uncle Joseph ever tell you not to read them?"

"I wish he had! I know well enough he does not like me to read them, but he never absolutely forbade me. I believe I should not have touched them if he had said right out, 'Percy, I *forbid* it.' Once or twice I have wished I was in Ellerton's shoes when we have been changing the books. He makes no bones about it, but says his father has positively forbidden him to read anything of the sort; so that's an end to it, and the fellows don't offer to lend him any now. I might have been like you, Bruey, by now, if it had not been for those nasty books putting it all out of my head after that Sunday evening. It made one feel deceitful too. Do you recollect one night when you thought there were robbers?"

"Yes, I remember wondering you were not interested about it. That night puzzled me very much, for I felt sure I saw a light under your door, and then it went out."

"So there was. I was reading, not thinking of anything else, and I pushed the book a little, and it sent my desk over on the floor. I had set it on the very edge of the table, and it came down with such a thump I guessed it must be heard; so as soon as I had seen that it was right side up, I turned the gas off, and kept as still as a dead mouse. That was a specimen. And when a fellow feels he is doing wrong, it is no end harder to get right."

"When one feels one has done wrong, dear Per, one wants to come to Jesus to be forgiven. And He will forgive. You know one of the children's back texts was, '*The blood of Jesus Christ His Son cleanseth us from all sin.*' But I wish you would never read any more of those books now you know they do you no good."

Percy gave a sort of laugh, which implied that she did not know how strong the temptation was. "Easier said than done," he said.

"You said it would have been easier if your papa had forbidden it out and out?"

"So it would."

"Well, don't you think it would make it easier still if you were quite sure you were disobeying God Himself?"

"You are a good hand at texts, but I don't know where you will find one to forbid me reading these books."

"*Let us lay aside every weight!*" said Bruey, gravely. "That is plain enough. And it is written in God's Word. It seems to me quite as plain as if it mentioned the particular weight that hinders one, because it says '*every* weight.' And if those books kept you from seeking Jesus when you did feel a little inclined to do so, I think they must be a very great 'weight.' Could you not 'lay it aside' for Jesus' sake, Percy?"

"What are you smiling at?"

"I was thinking, supposing your eyes were opened some night, like Elisha's servant, and you could see the King in His beauty, so loving and so glorious, standing very near you, and calling you to come to Him, and promising to make you very happy, and to keep you safe for ever, if you would only shut your book and look up, and listen, and come to Him,—*would you go on reading?*"

Interruptions always come exactly when *we* would rather they did not; but as God orders everything, they must be part of His plan. Bruey had several other things to say to Percy; but if Mrs. Murray had not come in at that moment to take her up to bed, that last little appeal would not have been the last, and would not perhaps have sunk into his memory and influenced his life as they did.

He took Bruey's place on the sofa when she was gone, and kicked less than was his wont during the twilight half-hour which followed.

Next morning no prayer-bell rang. He came downstairs, and found no one in the dining-room. There was a ring at the hall-door bell, and a gentleman's voice in the hall, and, soon after, a tread overhead, which was not Mrs. Murray's. He went in search of Alice. "Yes, Miss Bruey was very ill, and she had been down to Rilverton to fetch the doctor." But she knew no more than this. He wandered restlessly about, till he heard the doctor's foot on the stairs, when he decamped into the dining-room again.

Presently Mrs. Murray came in, looking troubled indeed.

"Percy, you have had no breakfast, but I could not come before. Help yourself; never mind me."

And having poured out Percy's coffee, she poured out a cup for herself, and put a bit of toast in the saucer to take upstairs. That was quite enough breakfast for her on such a sorrowful morning. She did not volunteer any information, and Percy did not like to ask. He could *see* that Bruey must be ill. But as she was leaving the room, he jumped up to open the door for her, and said, "Aunt, is she very ill?"

"We hardly know yet, Percy dear. Dr. Hawkins is afraid rheumatic fever is beginning, and with that poor little heart of hers."——She did not finish the sentence; neither did he finish his breakfast.

He was to go by the 10.50 train. The interval would have been intolerable but for the little final arrangements of his carpet-bag, which contained principally various precious boy-rubbish, his aunt having done the serious packing for him overnight. Before half-past ten he was quite ready, and hovering about the landing, wondering if he dared knock at Mrs. Murray's door, where all was very quiet. Presently the door was opened very softly, and she came out.

"She is dozing now, dear boy, and I must not wake her, she has been so feverish and ill all night. I will say good-bye for you when she wakes."

"Aunt, need I go?" said Percy. "Can't I be of any use? Go for medicines and things? I'd do anything in the world I could. Let me stop. I'll go and telegraph to papa."

"No, no, Percy dear. You had better go. You would soon be tired of it," she said, smiling sadly.

"Rheumatic fever is very long and trying; and it is not the first time."

"I really wish you would let me stay, Aunt. I know boys are supposed to be of no earthly use, but you should see. I believe I could be better than nothing. Don't let me go!"

He was thoroughly in earnest, and pleaded hard; but Mrs. Murray felt she could give more undivided attention to Bruey if he were gone; so she did not yield. His good-bye kiss was unusually tender; after it he hesitated, and cleared his throat, and at last got out—"Give my best love to Bruey, and tell her I won't forget. She'll know! Good-bye again, Aunt."

CHAPTER XIV.

VERY HARD WORK.

BRUEY'S work for the next few weeks was very hard indeed. It consisted of trying to be still when she felt strangely restless, or trying to move a very little bit without making the pain much worse; and trying to keep from fretting when she felt very low, and to keep from moaning when the pain was very wearying, partly that she might not add to her mamma's trouble, and partly because she felt more clearly than ever before that she was really a little servant of Christ, and therefore wished to follow His example and obey His commands more than ever before. Yes, it was very hard work indeed. And it grew harder in one way,—there was more suffering instead of less as time went on, for the pain, that began to be more frequent and oppressive at the heart, was worse to bear than the worst aching of the limbs; but easier in another,—for the promise, "*My grace is sufficient for thee*" was not only for that great servant of Christ, St. Paul, but for every servant of Christ, even if they happen to be little girls of twelve years old. And she found the truth of it now that she needed grace to suffer. Sweet thoughts of Him came more often; sweet verses came into her mind; and without exactly *thinking* about them, for she was too tired to think, they seemed to float on her heart, and hush it and gladden it all through the long nights.

Only once or twice came a day when the Enemy, who could not harm the little lamb which trusted itself to the Good Shepherd's keeping, seemed allowed to distress her. It was worse than pain when a terrible doubt came, whether she was safe in Jesus, and when recollections of all sorts of forgotten naughtiness suddenly started up, and recollections of carelessness about Him and forgetfulness of Him over and over again, even after she fancied she had begun to love Him; and when she wondered whether she ever really loved Him at all, and whether it had not all been a mistake, and she a little hypocrite all the time. This did not last long. The tender Shepherd, who had some wise reason for permitting it, soon cleared away the clouds, and drew her to rest again in His forgiveness and unchanging love. How little she thought, when she made her little class repeat over and over again the "back texts," till they knew them as well as their own names, that those very texts would come to her in her weakness and need, and bring light and strength and happiness, when she could hardly have taken in any less familiar words. So it was that after one of these dark days the words—"*The blood of Jesus Christ His Son cleanseth us from all sin*"—came into her heart as something so true and so strong, that every doubt fled away before it. Another time the first text she ever taught her little girls came like a message from Himself, and hushed every fear. It was only eight words altogether, and it was only four of these that won the battle, the last battle, for Bruey—"*He first loved us!*" She never doubted His love again after that day.

The warm weather returned, and Bruey's petition that Willie Fosbery might come, without waiting till she was better, could not be refused. Of course, it was a damper upon his delight that Miss Bruey could not come down to see him; but he did not realise how ill she was, so he had an amount of enjoyment out of his day under the great tree which would be something to live upon for weeks, not to mention the good that a day's fresh air seemed to do him. Miss Allison came and had a little talk with him, and brought him some strawberries and a book of pictures, and a kind message from Bruey.

When Alice took him home, she decided that he ought to stop at Mrs. Madingley's door on the way, and thank her in person for the use of the perambulator. After some shy objections, he consented, but Alice must be spokeswoman.

Mrs. Madingley stepped out to speak to him, or rather to look at him, for it was not much in her line to enter into benevolent conversations. "Willie wishes to thank you, Ma'am," said Alice, "for your kindness in lending us the perambulator; don't you, Willie?"

"I thank you, Ma'am," said Willie, formally, touching his cap.

"He was quite welcome," she said, looking at him as if he were a harmless specimen from a wild beast show. "So this is the little boy Miss Murray goes to see. Was it an accident?"

Willie frowned. He disliked inquiries or remarks. Alice answered, "No, Ma'am, he never walked. It's very bad for him, Ma'am; the time used to seem so long to him; but he has been much better since Miss Murray took to be kind to him." Willie smiled a confirmation of this.

"He looks pale," remarked Mrs. Madingley.

"Please, Ma'am, he looks as well again as he did this morning. It has done you good, hasn't it, Willie? He had not been out of our yard for three years."

"And I should not have been out for three years more, maybe, if it had not been for Miss Murray," said Willie. "There's no one to take me now; I'm too big to be carried like a baby."

Mrs. Madingley looked rather surprised to hear the specimen make a remark. "Then you enjoyed it?" she said.

Willie gave her an odd, half-contemptuous glance, as if she might have known better than to ask such a question, or use such a feeble term. "If you saw our yard, you would see. There is no grass and no tree, only stones. And *hot!*" But he recollected his manners in time to finish his speech with, "Yes, Ma'am, I *did* enjoy it." The interview was ended by a sixpence finding its way into Willie's hand. Mrs. Madingley went back into the house, and the words "three years" followed her. "Only stones. And *hot!*" for three whole summers; while her precious little ones had grass, and trees, and flowers, and fresh air every day. What an odd child that Bruey Murray was to think of borrowing her perambulator! But it was a very good idea, all the same; and it was not unpleasant to reflect that, without any trouble or expense to herself, she had enabled this poor cripple boy to have one summer day in a garden instead of "our yard." But it was Bruey's idea!

Bruey was rather better that evening, and able to receive Alice's report of Willie's safe return. It had been a wonderful pleasure to her to think of her little scheme having come to pass, and poor Willie really having a long day under trees again.

Alice had justified her character of being handy, so, in hope of Jane's possible return, no other servant was engaged, and she stayed on. Mrs. Fayling came now and then to help down stairs, but Alice had the waiting on Mrs. Murray and Bruey, and was often left alone in the room with the invalid for a short time—not for very long, for Mrs. Murray was never away longer than she could help. Bruey was too ill for much conversation, but now and then a little word was said which Alice never forget. Still this was seldom, and the chief thing which day by day told upon Alice, was the patient quiet bearing of what she knew must be great pain by the remedies used; and still more the very expression of Bruey's face, and the tone of her voice, about which she too noticed and felt that indescribable "something," which had so touched and quieted Percy. She was an intelligent girl, well up in Sunday-school lessons, and ready with answers to any questions about the Children of Israel or the journeys of St. Paul, and could tell you what justification and sanctification meant. But she could come home from school and pin flowers in her hat, or arrange for a walk with giddy girls. She came out of Bruey's room night after night, when the last little services had been rendered, inclined to kneel very quietly down by her bedside, and turn some of the things she knew so well into prayer. And when Miss Bru-ey asked her, as she sometimes did, for a text, it was strange how startlingly real and true the words sounded to herself as she repeated them. Yet they were the very same which she had gabbled off in class, with no thought or wish about them but to make sure of getting the best mark for her lesson. So Bruey was do-ing work for Jesus without knowing it, as she lay through that long July, never once leaving her room.

One evening she asked her mamma to move her a little more to the other side of the bed. It was done.

"And now, Mamma, please set the dressing-room door wide open."

Then she lay, with a contented smile, looking through the opening. "I can see my own corner now, Mamma."

Not much to see, it would seem; but how was the happy smile to be ac-counted for? Recollections of twilight hours in that corner rose up, dimly at first, then more clearly, but always sweetly, and always twining round the words, "*There will I meet with thee.*" Now it seemed as if He had always met her there, only that she knew it not. "*There!*" Yes, He had kept the promise. The old box, and the little table, and the window sill, all witnessed it. "*There!*" And they faded out of sight somehow, for the eyes closed, and the heart flew up on that word "*There*" to a land very far off and yet very near, and she seemed to be straining through a haze of golden glory and a maze of enfolding music, to see One Face and to hear One Voice. And then a bright cloud overshadowed her, but she was *not* afraid; and the music all melted away into a soft chiming of bells like St. Mary's, only sweeter; and they said, "*Thine eyes shall see the King! Thine eyes shall see the King!*" and up above them another peal kept ringing, very far away, but very clear, "*In His beauty! In His beauty!*" And the chime below and the peal above blended and mingled in peace and love. And she lay with that happy smile on her face. Surely that room was a holy place!

"Hush, Alice, she is asleep!" whispered her mother. "She will be better when she wakes."

CHAPTER XV.

REST.

IT was a calm sunny day of the first week in August, the last of the summer holidays at Rilverton Grammar School, where the new-fangled "terms" had not yet
been adopted. Bruey's room was very quiet, though it had another occupant.
Ada Murray had come home from her foreign school, and helped to nurse her
little suffering sister. Miss Elizabeth Allison had helped too, more than once
staying a whole night while Mrs. Murray tried to rest in another room.

On this day Bruey did not seem to want anything. It felt like a pleasant rest
after some days and nights of more than common pain and restlessness. She
dozed a good deal, and when she was awake lay placidly, very, very tired, but
very happy, hardly ever speaking, but now and then smiling as her eye caught
her mother's or Ada's. Only several times she whispered, when Ada was very
near her, "What time?" And when Ada told her, she would smile again, and
shut her eyes.

Percy was coming that evening. Uncle Joseph hardly knew what to do
about his returning when his cousin was so ill; but Mrs. Murray wrote that she
had been looking forward so much to it, and so counting the days till his return,
that the little excitement of seeing him would be less harm than the disappoint-
ment if he did not come, or if it was arranged for him to board elsewhere for a
while. And though dear Bruey was very ill, she was not hopelessly so; still her
recovery must be a very long one.

But on the morning of this day another note came to say that she had been
much worse, and that she was very anxious for Percy's coming; so that, if he
could come by an earlier train, it would be a relief. The letters were a little late
at Mr. Murray's country home, and this made it impossible to catch the morning train at the nearest station, which was several miles off; so Percy had to wait
for the mid-day train, as previously intended. The journey seemed long and

wearisome. He compared his watch with every station clock of which he could catch sight, and it really seemed as if there were a conspiracy between them all along the line to go slow.

At last, as the sun was pouring almost level rays through the glowing tree-trunks, the train slackened speed and ran into a tunnel, coming slowly out among the trucks and sidings and points of a large station. He had everything in his hands, ready to spring out as soon as the train ran up to the platform. He hailed a porter before it stopped, committed his luggage to him, and started off by a short cut which would take him to Calton Terrace in less time than a cab could go by the road.

He did not think his cousin could be going to die; it was not that which made him hasten; he could not have said what it was, only a restless longing to get there, as soon as possible. He checked himself as he came nearer; why should he race like that? It was very quiet along the terrace; almost every one was gone from home, and no one was about. Something made him dislike even the crunching of his feet on the gravel, and he walked along the rim of grass which ran outside the railing of the little gardens. The door of No. 8 was open. He went in. It was quiet here too. He went softly upstairs. Mrs. Murray's room door was ajar. He stepped inside, so softly that no one heard him. Mrs. Murray sat with her back to him; Ada, tired with the long day's watching, and a broken night before it, had leant her head on the bed and closed her eyes. But he hardly saw them. There lay dear Bruey, quietly asleep, as it seemed; not much changed, but the "something" which he felt last time he saw her, had brightened and grown into a look of such strong and heavenly peace that no one would ever need to prove to him that religion was a reality, and God's peace a reality, and triumph over sin and death a reality. The sun poured in below the nearly closed blind, and a bright band of light lay upon her hand. It was resting lightly on the white quilt, with the forefinger pointing towards the open door of the dressing-room; and across the little table lay another band of sunlight. He saw it all, and recollected it all afterwards; but whether he stood watching the scene for seconds or minutes he could not have told.

Suddenly Mrs. Murray looked round. An expression of fear and distress came over her face as she started to see Percy standing there. She motioned him to go away, signing to the little sleeper to show her fear lest she should wake and be startled at seeing him, and perhaps suffer for it. But she need not have feared. Before Percy could move away, Bruey opened her eyes with a smile, and said, "Percy! Come!" as calmly as if he had been beside her when she closed them. Percy came forward, and kissed her. She motioned to Ada, who, following her hint, drew her dear old Bible from under her pillow, and laid it close to the sunlit hand. That little hand had just strength left to raise itself and rest upon it, and the sweet lips whispered, "Percy's!" He knelt, and took the little hand in his, and bowed his head over it, and the band of sunlight lay upon both together; and there was a hush.

Did Another come, unheard, unseen, save by one, into that quiet room? It was no sunlight that fell upon the little sweet face, more beautiful now than ever in its rosy health, for the broad band narrowed and faded away as Percy again raised his head, and saw the sweet eyes open once more, never so bright as now—never so bright as when they looked up with a wonderful smile of glad surprise and welcome, and the words passed the parted lips, "*His beauty!*" Then they closed again; there was no struggle, only one long sigh, and dear little Bruey was at rest, her eyes beholding "*the King in His beauty*," her short work on earth all ended, and the joy of her Lord entered.

Dear little Bruey! We thought she would grow up to be such a useful "worker for Christ"; but her work was begun and ended in less than one year. Yet not "ended"; for "*His servants shall serve Him*" not only here, where we can do so little for the Lord Jesus, though we would like to do so much; when we are "*with Him*" for ever, I think He will give us something to do for Him. Who knows what holy and beautiful work dear little Bruey is doing for Him now!

And who knows where even the little work she began upon earth will end! how the texts she taught may spring up and bear fruit in the lives of her little girls, and perhaps come back to them in comfort and blessing when they are old women! How some of the forty-one names on her Irish cards became steady subscribers and friends of that cause; and how dark, sad hearts in far-away Irish glens may have been made to sing for joy, and then to cause others to sing for joy, by the sweet story of peace taught them by means of many a "five shillings" which would never have reached Dublin but for her! How different Percy's life might have been but for "that Sunday evening!" How that "something," of which Bruey herself was unconscious, and which neither of them could explain, woke thoughts and feelings in Alice which never died away! How poor Willie's weary little life was linked to a brighter life beyond! And how the account of her patient suffering, and of her peaceful falling asleep, touched the hearts of every one who had known her, and spoke more strongly of the reality of faith and hope in Christ than any living words could have done! Dear little Bruey! her work is indeed not "ended."

But there is work for many another "little worker for Christ." Who will say, "*Lord, here am I, send me*"?

POSTSCRIPT.

ONE part of dear little Bruey's work has borne a great deal of fruit,—her Irish collecting. Not a few have wished to have a "green card" after reading her story. And now the Irish Society has a "Bruey Branch," which we hope will be a very fruitful one.

Who will join it? Who will send for a green card, and set to work as a "Bruey Collector"? Do not fancy, because you are not likely to get as many names as she did, that it is not worth trying at all. Don't you think you could get five shillings? And you know that will teach *one* to read the Bible. Don't you know *anybody* who would give sixpence to begin with?

Our "Bruey Branch" has a motto—"For Jesus' sake *only!*" For I do not want you to collect for Bruey's sake, but for His sake only; and then your work will be blessed, and you will be blessed in doing it. Then all the golden fruit of the Bruey Branch will be really "fruit unto God," and "fruit unto life eternal."

Send your name to Mr. Henry Maguire, 17 Upper Sackville Street, Dublin, and he will send you a card just like Bruey's, and a report by which you can see what the other Bruey Collectors are doing. And next year I hope we shall have doubled our numbers, for the need is far greater now than even when dear Bruey was at work.

F. R. H.

A.D. 33.

said, I *ª* go unto the Father: for my *ᵇ* Father is greater than I. *J. 17. 5. He. 2. 7. m*

29 And now I have told you before it come to pass, that, when it is come to pass, ye might believe.

30 Hereafter I will not talk much with you: for the prince *ᶠ* of this world cometh, and hath nothing *ᵍ* in me.

31 But, that the world may know that I love the Father; and as *ʰ* the Father gave me commandment, even so I do. Arise, let us go hence.

CHAPTER XV.

I AM the true vine, *ⁱ* and my Father is the husbandman. *ᵏ*

2 Every branch *ᵐ* in me that beareth not fruit he taketh away: and every branch that beareth *ᵒ* fruit, he purgeth it, that it may bring forth more fruit. *⁊⁊. 41. 3⁊*

3 Now ye *ᵖ* are clean through the word which I have spoken unto you. *⁊ 115, 11 c 13. 10*

4 Abide *ᵗ* in me, and I in you. As *ᵘ* the branch cannot bear fruit of itself, except it abide in the vine; no more can ye, except ye abide in me.

5 I am the vine, ye *are* the branches: He that abideth in me, and I in him, the same bringeth forth much fruit: for *ᵞ* without me ye can do nothing.

6 If a *ᵂ* man abide not in me, he is cast forth as a branch, and is withered; and men gather them, and cast *them* into the fire, and they are burned.

7 If ye abide in me, and my words abide in you, ye *ᶻ* shall ask what ye will, and it shall be done unto you. *Rob. 1. 4. 174.*

8 Herein is my Father glorified, that ye bear much fruit; so shall ye be my disciples.

9 As the Father hath loved me, so have I loved you: continue ye in my love.

10 If ye *ᵃ* keep my commandments, ye shall abide in my love; even as I have kept my Father's commandments, and abide in his love.

11 These things have I spoken unto you, that my joy might remain in you, and that your *ᶜ* joy might be full.

12 This *ᵈ* is my commandment, That ye love one another, as I have loved you.

13 Greater love *ᵉ* hath no man than this, that a man lay down his life for his friends.

14 Ye *ʰ* are my friends, if ye do whatsoever I command you. *Jas. 1. 18.*

15 Henceforth I call you not servants; for the servant knoweth not what his lord doeth: but I have called you friends: *ⁱ* for all things that I have heard of my Father I have made known unto you. *Ge. 18. 17*

16 Ye *ᵏ* have not chosen me, but I have chosen you, and ordained *ᵖ* you, that ye should go and bring forth fruit, and *that* your fruit should remain: that whatsoever ye shall ask of the Father in my name, he may give it you.

17 These things *ⁱ* I command you, that ye love one another.

18 If the world *ᵏ* hate you, ye know that it hated me before *it hated* you.

19 If ye were of the world, the world would love his own: but because ye are not of the world, but I have chosen you *ᵒ* out of the world, therefore *ᵖ* the world hateth you.

20 Remember *ᵍ* the word that I said unto you, The servant is not greater than his lord. If they have persecuted me, they will also persecute you; if they *ᵐ* have kept my saying, they will keep your's also.

ª verse 12.
ᵇ 1 Co. 15. 27, 28.
ᶜ chap. 16. 3. Mat. 10. 23. 24. 9.
ᵈ chap. 9. 41.
ᵉ Ja. 4. 17.
β or, excuse.
ᶠ chap. 16. 11. Ep. 2. 2.
ᵍ 2 Co. 5. 21. He. 4. 15. 1 John 3. 5.
ʰ Ps. 40. 8. Phi. 2. 8.
ⁱ chap. 7. 31.
ⱼ Is. 4. 2.
ᵏ Ca. 8. 12.
ˡ Ps. 35. 19. 69. 4.
ᵐ Mat. 15. 13.
ⁿ chap. 14. 17.
ᵒ He. 12. 15. Re. 3. 19.
ᵖ 1 John 5. 6.
ᵍ chap. 17. 17. Ep. 5. 26. 1 Pe. 1. 22.
ʳ Lu. 24. 43. Ac. 2. 32. 2 Pe. 1. 16.
ˢ 1 John 1. 2.
ᵗ 1 John 2. 6.
ᵘ Ho. 14. 8. Ga. 2. 20. Phi. 1. 11.
ᵛ Ac. 26. 9...11.
y or, severed from me.
ᵂ Mat. 3. 10. 7. 19.
ˣ chap. 15. 21.
ʸ 1 Co. 2. 8. 1 Ti. 1. 13.
ᶻ chap. 16. 23 c 14. 21. 23.
ᵇ verse 22.
ᶜ chap. 16. 24. 17. 13.
δ or, convince, Ac. 2. 37.
ᵈ chap. 13. 34.
ᵉ Ro. 5. 7, 8.
ᶠ Ro. 3. 20.
ᵍ Is. 42. 21. Ro. 1. 17.
ʰ verse 10.
ⁱ Ac. 17. 31. Ro. 2. 2. Re. 20. 12, 13.
ᵏ chap. 12. 31.
ˡ Ja. 2. 23.
ᵐ He. 5. 12.
ᵒ 1 Jno. 4. 10, 19.
ᵖ Ep. 2. 10.
ᵍ Re. 1. 1, 19.
ʳ verse 7.
ᵃ chap. 14. 13.
ˢ verse 12.
ᵗ 1 Jno. 3. 13.
ᵘ chap. 17. 14.
ᵛ chap. 13. 16. Mat. 10. 24. Lu. 6. 40.
ᵂ Eze. 3. 7.

---

21 But all *ᵉ* these things will they do unto you for my name's sake, because they know not him that sent me.

22 If I *ᵈ* had not come and spoken unto them, they had not had sin: but *ᵉ* now they have no *β* cloke for their sin. *Ro. 1. 20, 9. 19*

23 He that hateth me hateth my Father also.

24 If I had not done among them the works *ⁱ* which none other man did, they had not had sin: but now have they both seen and hated both me and my Father.

25 But *this cometh to pass*, that the word might be fulfilled that is written in their law, They hated *ⁱ* me without a cause.

26 But when the Comforter *ᵏ* is come, *c. 16. 7,* whom I will send unto you from the Father, *c. 14. 26, even* the Spirit of truth, which proceedeth from the Father, he *ᵐ* shall testify of me:

27 And ye *ⁿ* also shall bear witness, because ye *ᵒ* have been with me from the *Lu. 22. 28* beginning.

CHAPTER XVI.

THESE things I spoken unto you, that ye should not be offended.

2 They shall put you out of the synagogues: yea, the time cometh, that whosoever *ˣ* killeth you will think that he doeth God service.

3 And these *ʸ* things will they do unto you, because they *ᶻ* have not known the Father, nor me.

4 But these things have I told you, that when the time shall come, ye may remember that I told you of them. And these *ª* things I said not unto you at the beginning, because I was with you.

5 But now I go my way unto him that sent me; and none of you asketh me, Whither goest thou?

6 But because I have said these things unto you, sorrow *ᵇ* hath filled your heart.

7 Nevertheless I tell you the truth; It *Lu. 24* is expedient for you that I go away: for *⁊/ 11.* if I go not away, the Comforter will not come unto you; but if I depart, I will send him unto you. *c. 15. 26*

8 And when he is come, he will *ᵇ* reprove the world of sin, and of righteousness, and of judgment:

9 Of sin, *ᶠ because* they believe not on me; *c. 3. 36.*

10 Of righteousness, *ᵍ* because I go to my Father, and ye see me no more;

11 Of judgment, *ⁱ* because *ᵏ* the prince of this world is judged. *c. 12. 31. No. 9. 11.*

12 I have yet many things to say unto *Lu. 7. 40* you, but ye *ᵐ* cannot bear them now. *c. 6. 60. ᵛ 9*

13 Howbeit when he, the Spirit of truth, *Jno. 3. 3.* is come, he *ⁿ* will guide you into all truth: *Is. 30. 10* for he shall not speak of himself; but *Mar. 4. 35* whatsoever he shall hear, *that* shall he speak: and he *ʳ* will shew you things to come.

14 He shall glorify me: for he shall receive of mine, and shall shew *it* unto you. *2 Co. 11. 4.*

15 All things that the Father hath are *Lu. 10. 22* mine: therefore said I, that he shall take *c. 7. 16* of mine, and shall shew *it* unto you.

16 A little while, and ye shall not see me: and again, a little while, and ye shall see me, because I go to the Father.

17 Then said *some* of his disciples among themselves, What is this that he saith unto us, A little while, and ye shall not see me: and again, a little while, and ye shall see me: and, Because I go to the Father?

18 They said therefore, What is this that he saith, A little while? we cannot tell what he saith.

77

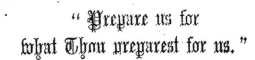

"Prepare us for what Thou preparest for us."

"Prepare our selves for what, O Lord,
　Thou dost for us prepare!"
A dying mother taught her child
　To breathe the little prayer:

A God - sent word the mother left,
　A widely - bearing seed;
Heart after heart pours forth her prayer
　Against its hour of need.

Prepare us, Lord, for every task
　Thou givest us to do;
Prepare us for the tangled ways
　We have to struggle through.

Prepare us, lest in happier days
　We try alone to go,
Forgetting then to seek the hand
　We cry for in our woe.

"Experience teaches!" True, but life
　Doth ne'er itself repeat;
Each trial, new in something, proves
　Our training incomplete.

Thou know'st, but feebly can we work,
　But weakly can we bear;
At best we struggle blindly on:
　Our lot and us prepare!

Make us more ready to perceive,
　More strong to do Thy will,
That soul and body Thy commands
　May cheerfully fulfil.

And when, our life - probation o'er,
　We lie too faint for prayer,
O Saviour, speak those gracious words,
　"Thy mansion I prepare."

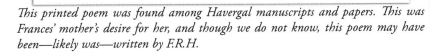

This printed poem was found among Havergal manuscripts and papers. This was Frances' mother's desire for her, and though we do not know, this poem may have been—likely was—written by F.R.H.

Frances Ridley Havergal was 15 in April, 1852, when this poem was written. She was 11 when her mother, Jane Head Havergal, died on July 5, 1848. This poem was never published in Frances' lifetime, and was found only in her handwritten manuscript.

A mother's loss! Oh who may tell
Its anguish, or what power can quell
The deepest grief, most heartfelt woe
Which childhood's sunny hours may
                              [know.
Ah! childhood's happy days are past
In mirth and glee; no shades are cast
Upon their bright and happy way
Where sunbeams ere around them play.

No cares have they: the floweret sweet
Springs up to cheer their tiny feet.
Their tears are like the gentle dew
Which brighten still that floweret's hue.

E'en if a cloud appears awhile
To dim their merry gleeful smile,
A rainbow will be planted there
In colours bright and passing fair.

And music dwells in childhood's voice
Which can the weary heart rejoice.

Its merry tones as blithely ring
As birds which welcome early spring.
                              [crowned
And joy that fair young head hath
As with a garland circling round,
Bright are the flowerets which compose
That wreath of joy untouched by woe.

But brightest of the blossoms there
And fairest of those flowerets fair,
That priceless gift from God above
In mercy sent: a mother's love.
                              [severed,
That flower from childhood's bosom
Its sweetest gift is gone for ever.
The wreath of joy! Oh how defaced!
How can that loss e'er be replaced.

Torn is that young and tender heart
When called from mother love to part.
Ah! manhood stern can never know
The depth of this its bitterest woe!

                    F.R.H. 1852

William Henry Havergal (1793–1870), Frances Ridley Havergal's father. This was painted by Solomon Cole in 1845.

Jane Head Havergal (1794?–1848), Frances' mother, painted by Solomon Cole in 1845. Frances was 11 when she died.

Frances Ridley Havergal (1836–1879). Solomon Cole painted this portrait in 1845, when she was eight years old.

THE

FOUR HAPPY DAYS.

BY

FRANCES RIDLEY HAVERGAL,

Author of "Bruey," "Under the Surface," "Ministry of Song," "Under His Shadow," "My King," etc., etc.

SIXTH EDITION.

LONDON:
JAMES NISBET AND CO., BERNERS STREET.
1880.

CONTENTS.

The Four Happy Days.

CHAPTER I.

"MARCH at last! I wish it was April. No; I wish it was May!" said Annie. "Oh dear, what a long time it takes to get to the end of a month!"

She said it to a lady who had lately come to live in her father's parish, and to whom she had taken a great fancy, partly because she was so very kind and pleasant, and partly because she would sometimes leave the grown-up people and have what Annie called "a nice talk" with her, submitting to be asked questions by the dozen about all sorts of things, great and small, which Annie "wanted to know about," and which never came in her lesson-books. Miss Allen laughed at this great grievance of the long months, which had once or twice before been spoken of in the same tone.

"You ought not to complain now; February finished two or three days sooner than any other month, and yet you are not a bit grateful. But, Annie, why are you in such a hurry to get through the months? They go too fast for me instead of too slowly. I am glad you have not the managing of them."

"Because I want my four happy days to come, and none of them come for so long yet."

"Your four happy days? I thought none of your days were particularly unhappy; but what are these special ones? I have never heard about them yet."

"Then I'll tell you, may I? Can you stay? Oh, it's so nice to have you all to myself! I hope nobody will come in just directly." And Annie settled herself on a foot-stool by Miss Allen, holding one of her hands in both her own, stroking and fondling it as if it were a pussy, while she gave her explanation.

"I looked in the almanacs as soon as we got them, to see when the first of my four happy days would come. I could have found it in the Prayer-book, only I did not think of it in time. The others I knew without, quite well. It is Whit-Monday, and that is why I want the end of May to be here. You have not been with us on a Whit-Monday yet, and you can't think how nice it is! All the Sunday schools go to the cathedral in the morning; the nave is quite filled: I go with my own class, and sit with them. Then we come back and have the school feast, and I help to hand the cake; and then all the rewards are given, and we have ever so much singing—such lovely things, you have not heard them yet; and then the boys cheer for the Queen, and for Papa, and for some other people, and the girls clap; they do make such a noise—it is such fun! Oh, I am so happy that day! And I forgot, that is not all. We decorate the room early in the morning, and the cake is made the Saturday before, and all the reward books are in the house for several days, and I may have them to read. Do you know little Mary Passey in my class,—the tiny child, with funny little black eyes? I think she will get the best book in the class next Whit-Monday. Now, do be at home for it; don't go out on a visit just then, please."

"Well, I will not if I can help it," said Miss Allen. "I think this first happy day sounds very pleasant. What is the second?"

"Oh, the second is the 18th of July. You could not guess why that is one, so I'll tell you. It is little Louie's birthday—my niece. Don't laugh, now, Miss Allen; it's too bad: why should not I have a niece as well as other people? I was an aunt when I was only six years old, and now I am eleven. Well, I always go to Elmerton for her birthday, and stay a week or two at least. You know she is the only one, and they always keep her birthday. All the labourers' wives and children come to dinner in the servants' hall, and I dare say they will have a party afterwards. Then I go rides on the pony when I am at Elmerton, and my great friend Katie comes to stay with me. Am I tiring you, Miss Allen? But I want to tell you the others, if you don't mind. There is a long time to wait from the second to the third happy day,—nearly four months; it is the 5th of November. We can't have bonfires in a town, you know; but more than two years ago Maria Silter and I made a capital plan for keeping it. We begin in August, and ask all our friends to give us something, sixpences and threepenny bits, and sometimes we get shillings. I keep the accounts, and we call it the 'Flannel Petticoat Society.' As soon as we have got enough, we go and buy some flannel, but we don't stop collecting till the end of October. (Oh, Miss Allen, would you give me something for it next August? No; will you really? A shilling! Oh, you *are* a darling!) What was I telling you?—oh, about the flannel. One of my sisters or one of hers goes with us to get it, and then we set to work and make as many flannel petticoats (all ourselves) as we can get money for. Last year we made twenty-nine. Then my sisters help me to make a list of the children who are to have them, and they come to the rectory for them on the 5th of November. It is such fun measuring them. We run tucks in, because the flannel shrinks, you know, when it is washed. Then we give each child a piece of cake, and make them sing; then Maria stays to tea with me. I daresay we shall make more than thirty petticoats this year. I can work faster now, and it seems to me one can always do everything better every year than we could the year before; doesn't it seem so to you, Miss Allen?"

"I wish it did, Annie dear! But what is the fourth happy day?"

"That is the only one I do not know exactly about; it is my birthday, the 16th of December. You see, I can't tell beforehand what presents I shall have, nor what birthday treat I shall have—perhaps Maria will come to tea; but, anyhow, it will be my birthday. So these are my four happy days; and I should think you don't wonder now that I want this stupid March and April to be done with, do you? Miss Allen, dear, what is the matter?" And Annie's merry eager face changed as she saw Miss Allen looking down on her so lovingly, yet, somehow, so sadly, that it almost startled her. Miss Allen put the hand of which Annie had not taken possession upon her head, and did not speak for a minute, during which Annie looked up into her face in wondering and rather unusual silence.

"Annie, dear, what if the happy days never come for you? or what if they come, and yet are *not* happy days?"

"Oh, Miss Allen, Whit-Monday always comes; why, it's in the Prayer-book! And Louie's birthday can't be altered; and the 5th of November *must* be happy; and——" Just then the door opened softly, and a gentle and very delicate-looking young lady came in.

"She will be able to see you now, I think, if you like to come up-stairs, dear Jessie."

Miss Allen rose. "Thank you," she said; "I am so glad she is less suffering to-day. I have brought a few more flowers, Mary, dear; the last must be quite faded now." "Oh, how good of you!" said Mary. "Mamma does so enjoy them! I never saw an invalid value flowers so much." Then she turned to her little sister, and asked her to bring a certain little vase to her mamma's room. Annie trotted briskly away to fetch it, and then returned to her occupation of colouring a missionary map, much wishing that grown-up people would not always take such gloomy views of things; even Miss Allen, it seemed, was no better in this respect than others. What harm could it be to look forward to her four happy days?

JESUS, BLESSED SAVIOUR.

Tune—Hermas.

Words and Music by F. R. H.

Jesus, blessèd Saviour!
  Help us now to raise
Songs of glad thanksgiving,
  Songs of holy praise.

Oh, how kind and gracious
  Thou hast always been!
Oh, how many blessings
  Every day has seen!

Chorus—Jesus, blessèd Saviour!
  Now our praises hear,
For Thy grace and favour,
  Crowning all the year.

Jesus, holy Saviour!
  Only Thou canst tell
How we often stumbled,
  How we often fell!

All our sins (so many)!
  Saviour, Thou dost know:
In Thy blood most precious,
  Wash us white as snow.

Chorus—Jesus, blessèd Saviour!
  Keep us in Thy fear;
Let Thy grace and favour
  Pardon all the year.

Jesus, loving Saviour!
  Only Thou dost know
All that may befall us,
  As we onward go.

So we humbly pray Thee,
  Take us by the hand;
Lead us ever upward
  To the Better Land.

Chorus—Jesus, blessèd Saviour!
  Keep us ever near;
Let Thy grace and favour
  Shield us all the year.

Jesus, precious Saviour!
  Make us all Thine own;
Make us Thine for ever,
  Make us Thine alone!

Let each day, each moment,
  Of this glad New Year,
Be for Jesus only,—
  Jesus, Saviour dear!

Chorus—Then, O blessèd Saviour!
  Never need we fear,
For Thy grace and favour
  Crown our bright New Year.

CHAPTER II.

A T last March was gone, and April too, and May was come. The evenings grew longer and brighter every week, till Annie could go to bed in the twilight without any candle. She liked that, because it was a change. Besides, it was nice to go to sleep before it was quite dark, and her little room looked snug and pleasant till the very last, when she shut her eyes and said good-night to it.

That little room was a great thing to Annie. It was her consolation in leaving a pretty country home with a large garden, that in the town home she should have a room all to herself; and it went a long way towards making up for the loss. A funny little hole it was, with a ceiling that sloped down on one side almost to the edge of the bed. There was a little casement window, with a sill broad enough to serve as a table, and a blue curtain, which Annie could draw round her chair, and then she fancied herself in the cosiest little nest in the world. There were two shelves over the head of the bed, by the window, and these held all her own books and a few which had descended to her from elder sisters; so, when she awoke early in the summer mornings, they were nicely within reach, and she could read till it was time to get up. On the other side of the window was a chest of drawers, and by the foot of the bed a washstand, the door coming between them. The room would not hold any more, but this was quite enough; and if it had been any larger, it would not have been so cosy.

The view from the window was not beautiful, and yet it was better than nothing. All that could be seen near was old red brick, very smoky; except on one side, where one end of the church came in sight, and that was old grey stone, and very smoky too. But among the ugly warehouse walls and tiled roofs there was one little opening, and the window was high enough to get the benefit of it. That opening showed a little bit of real country, and a very pretty bit too; for it just faced Elbury, a hill with tall trees on the top, only a mile or two away. And the warehouses did not interfere much with the clouds, which had been Annie's great friends since she had had no trees to sit in and make up fancies about. Sometimes she watched them, and wondered all sorts of things about them, and especially wished she could reach the splendid white ones, which looked like snow mountains that could be climbed and rested upon. But she found in a book that they were only vapour like the others, and that there would be nothing to rest upon and look down from—only dismal thick mist and rain. Poor Annie! There are other bright things besides shining clouds which, when reached, are only mist and tears. Whit-Monday came and went, and its sunset found Annie kneeling on the chair, leaning her little arms on the window-seat, and feeling as if she wished she had something to lean her little heart on too. It had been a lovely day, and the school feast had been held as usual; and yet not quite as usual. Her papa had only been there part of the time; her sisters had only come in turn, each for an hour or two; the teachers seemed sad, and spoke very gently to Annie; and the children seemed to feel that something was different, and they were less merry than last Whit-Monday. There was a cloud upon the day, and it was worse and gloomier than the same cloud upon a common day, which was never expected to be so bright.

When Annie came home she had gone to her mamma's room, to tell her about Mary Passey's prize, and how Sarah Jones had broken her tea-cup, and how nice Alice Burton looked in the little jacket Mary had made for her, and sundry other pieces of news. But Mary met her at the door, and said very softly, "You must not chatter too fast this evening, Annie; Mamma cannot bear much. Don't stay long." So Annie had gone in saddened and subdued, and hardly told anything at all; and now she had come up to bed, and was musing over some words which had been spoken, and over the strange fact that Whit-Monday had come, and the feast had been held, and yet it had not been a very "happy day." The words were, "Annie, dear, pray to God to prepare you for all that He is preparing for you." Her mamma said them very feebly and solemnly when she said good-night, and now they seemed to sound over and over again, so that they never should or could be forgotten. "I wonder what He is preparing for me!" she thought. "Oh, I do hope He is preparing one of the many mansions for me! oh, I wish I knew whether He is! But I don't think He is preparing me for it, else I should not feel so naughty so often. Oh, I wish I were good! I wonder if I ever shall be. I wish I loved God. I know I ought, He is so good; I know that, and yet I don't feel as if I loved Him. Oh, I do wish I did!" Annie thought God was not preparing her, because she felt she was not prepared, and because she had begun to see that she did not love Him, and to wish very much that she did. Does any dear little girl who is reading this feel something like Annie? Dear child, listen, and do not hurry on with the story; but think about this for a minute or two, and perhaps it will help you and make you happier. Do not think, because you feel you are not good, and because you cannot say you love God and think how sad and wrong it is that you do not, and only wish you did love Him, that therefore He does not love you and care about you. If you feel this, and it makes you sorry, and you want to feel different, and to be like the people you know who do love the Lord Jesus and feel safe and happy, it is a sign that God's preparing you for what He is preparing for you. It is the Holy Spirit who is beginning to teach you His first lesson, which is, that you are a great sinner. Ask Him now to teach you the next lesson,—for it is a sweet and blessed one,—that the Lord Jesus is a great Saviour.

But Annie's mamma meant something besides this, something sadder and nearer, which she knew God was surely preparing day by day for her little girl. Annie could hardly remember the time when she had been *quite* well, but for more than a year she had been very ill, and always suffering pain. Now she was very weak indeed, and she knew that it could not be very long before she would be singing the "new song" in perfect joy, while all Annie's little songs would be hushed in great sorrow, the greatest that a child can know. And she perhaps prayed all the more that Annie might be prepared to bear it, because she saw how strangely unprepared she was for it. For it was strange. Though she saw so many sorrowful looks, and heard so many sad messages given to kind friends, and though she so often heard her mamma speak of going to heaven, and never of getting well, she would not believe, and did not believe, that she was going to die. There was a very wretched feeling which seemed to live down at the bottom of her heart, underneath everything else, that perhaps it *might* be true after all; but whenever this feeling came up, even for an instant, she smothered and hushed it down, and would not listen to it. "It can't be, and it won't be," she said to herself; "I am sure Mamma will soon be better; she is not so ill as she was last winter." And because she wished and tried hard to believe this, she really persuaded herself into believing it; and as she never would stay to listen to anything her sisters said about their dear mamma being worse, lest it should wake up this wretched feeling again, she succeeded at last in keeping it quiet and asleep. Yet all through these months, the dark, solemn shadow that rested on that sad and quiet rectory fell upon Annie's spirit too. God was gently preparing her by it, both for sorrow and for joy.

JESSIE'S FRIEND.

For Two Voices.

Words by F. R. H.
Music by Alberto Randegger.

Tenderly.

Little Jessie, darling pet,
  Do you want a Friend:
One who never will forget,
  Loving to the end;
One whom you can tell, when sad,
  Everything that grieves;
One who loves to make you glad;
  One who never leaves!

Such a loving Friend is ours,—
  Near us all the day;
Helping us in lesson hours,
  Smiling on our play;
Keeping us from doing wrong,
  Guarding everywhere;
Listening to each happy song,
  And each little prayer.

Jessie, if you only knew
  What He is to me,
Surely you would seek Him too,
  You would "Come and see."
Come, and you will find it true,
  Happy you will be;
Jesus says, and says to you,
  "Come! O come to Me!"

CHAPTER III.

JUNE came and went, and at last the 18th of July came, little Louie's birthday. But Annie was not at Elmerton, and little Louie had no birthday wreath and no birthday party that year. It was a sultry morning, hazy and hot; but it was not to keep out the heat that the blinds were all closed. Annie stood by the window in a front room at the top of the house, and looked into the street through the little space between the window-frame and the blind, which was not drawn quite straight. All the shops that she could see had their shutters up, and yet it was not Sunday. She had a new frock on that morning, but it was no pleasure to her: it was black—the first black dress she had ever worn. She knew it would be dreadful to look out of that window, and yet she felt as if she *must* look. She did not cry; she only stood and shivered in the warm air.

Very slowly and very quietly a funeral passed out of the little front gate, and in another minute was out of sight, turning into the church. Then Annie stood no longer, but rushed away to her own little room, and flung herself on her little bed, face down, and cried, "Oh, mamma! mamma! mamma!" It seemed as if there were nothing else in her little heart but that one word, and the great floods of tears that burst out with it. The strange hope which had lasted all that week was gone. She had found curious things in books, and one was, that people had sometimes been supposed to be dead and yet it was only a trance, and they had revived, and even recovered. The idea had possessed her that it might be so now, and again and again she had gone into the room when no one was near, and drawn the curtain aside, half-expecting to see the dear eyes unclose, and to feel the cold cheek warm again to her kiss. But it was no trance. The dear suffering mother was at rest, seeing Jesus face to face. Only the smile of holy peace was left upon her lips, and that remained to the last, telling of life beyond death; and this, perhaps, helped to keep Annie clinging to this wild hope. She had never seen the solemn beauty of that smile before. But now all hope was gone, utterly gone, and she *knew* that she was motherless. For a long time, she never knew how long, she lay sobbing, every now and then repeating that one word, never any other. She did not *think,*—she could not,—she only *felt.* No one came to her; she would not have spoken or moved if they had.

At last she fell asleep.

You will not want to hear more about that sorrowful day, so we will pass on to a happier one. But that was not the 5th of November. *That* passed almost unnoticed, and no "Flannel Petticoat Society" held its festival. After that sad 18th of July Annie and her sisters were away from home for a long time. Mary especially needed long rest and change of air. When they returned, Maria Silter was away; and there were reasons why it was thought better that for that year the little plan should be given up. Annie did not understand them, and at another time would have been bitterly disappointed, for nothing pleased her better than a little bustle and business. But under the shadow of her great sorrow she had learned to be more patient in lesser things, and so she said little about it. Besides, it was not like the year before, when each garment was shown to her dear mamma, and everything was talked about to her,—who was to have them, how much the flannel cost, and what new friend she had thought of asking for a donation to make up what was still wanted. So the 5th of November came and went, just as the other days did all through that weary autumn. Most people thought Annie's grief soon wore off, or rather that it had never been very deep at all for, just because it was deep, and did not wear off very soon, Annie did her utmost from the very first to conceal it. Not that it was always heavy upon her, for, if anything occupied her attention or caught her fancy, she had a happy faculty of entirely forgetting everything else for the moment, and throwing herself as completely into what was passing as if it were all the world to her. And thus it happened that a merry laugh would burst out, or a sudden light-heeled scamper up-stairs or down-stairs be made, which naturally led others to think that she could not have many sad thoughts; whereas not a minute before or after, the little heart would be as heavy as I hope not many little girls' hearts ever are.

Of all things, she dreaded hearing her beloved mother spoken of, partly because it seemed too sacred a subject for anyone to talk about, but chiefly because it brought up such a terrible flood of sorrow that she could not control herself. So, if she even guessed that anything was going to be said, she would instantly turn the subject so decidedly that it was impossible to come back to it; or, if alluded to in her hearing, she would slip out of the room in a moment. No one ever saw her cry after the first few days. But God did. He who said, "I have seen, I have seen," when His people were suffering in Egypt, saw all the tears that flowed when the blue curtain was drawn round the chair, and Annie leant her head on the window-seat in the autumn twilight, and did not even look up at the clouds.

TRUST.

For Two Voices.

Words by F. R. H.
Music by Alberto Randegger.

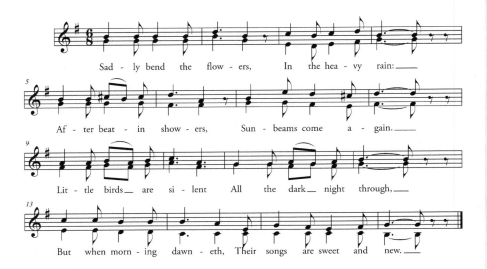

Sad - ly bend the flow - ers, In the hea - vy rain:
Af - ter beat - in show - ers, Sun - beams come a - gain.
Lit - tle birds are si - lent All the dark night through,
But when morn - ing dawn - eth, Their songs are sweet and new.

When a sudden sorrow
    Comes like cloud and night,
Wait for God's to-morrow,
    All will then be bright.
Only wait and trust Him
    Just a little while;
After evening tear-drops,
    Shall come the morning smile.

CHAPTER IV.

NOVEMBER was gone, and December came, and brought Annie's twelfth birthday. Could that be a happy day? Surely not,—the first birthday with no dear mamma's kiss! She did not expect that to be a happy day, and wished it were over.

All this time Miss Allen had often had "nice talks" with her, sometimes a few minutes, now and then a whole half-hour, and two or three times it had been more still, when Miss Allen had kindly taken Annie for a country walk, while her sisters were busy in their districts and schools. Miss Allen soon found out that Annie could not yet bear to have her great loss touched upon, and so she wisely and kindly waited till months, perhaps years, should soften it and make it less trying to her to hear the name spoken, less impossible to speak it herself to any human ear.

What were these talks about? Often they began merrily enough: Annie had funny little anecdotes to tell of the sayings and doings of her class, for the little children would tell her more than an older teacher could have got from them; or she was burning to describe some very interesting book which Maria Silter had lent her; or Miss Allen gave her a playful cross-examination about what she did all day, as she had such mere pretences of lessons; or made believe not to understand some of her accounts, and to be very stupid when Annie tried to explain in different ways what she meant; Annie in return pretending to be very impatient and cross with her, and yet of course enjoying it extremely. But, somehow, very often, and at last almost always, the talk became more serious and yet not less pleasant. Miss Allen had been a little child herself, like other people, but she had not, like most other people, forgotten how children feel, and what sort of thoughts pass through their minds, which they find it very hard to speak about to anyone. She believed, too, that in some ways they do not feel so very differently from grown-up people after all, and that many of the sad thoughts which she herself had known were very like some of Annie's, and that the same things which comforted her would comfort Annie, if only God opened her little heart to receive them.

And thus it was that, though she never asked Annie any questions, the child often wondered how Miss Allen could possibly know what she was thinking of, as over and over again she seemed to do. Miss Allen spoke about the words of the Lord Jesus to the woman of Samaria, "Whosoever drinketh of this water shall thirst again," and of what that meant; and Annie understood it quite well, because her happiest days had never seemed so perfectly happy as she had fancied them beforehand, and she knew very well what it was to feel something like thirst,—a wanting *something*, she could not tell what, but something that would fill her heart, and make her understand the words which follow,—"shall never thirst." Or if Miss Allen spoke of other words from the same gracious lips, of how He said, "Come unto me, all ye that are weary and heavy laden," Annie thought how glad she would be to come, because she knew what it was to feel weary and heavy laden. The blue curtain would have borne witness to that if it could have spoken, and so would the window-seat, on which the little arms so often leant in the twilight; yet she did not tell her friend all this. Only, if they were alone, and a pause came, Annie would nestle down by her, and lay her head on her lap, and say, "There, now, that's nice; now talk to me," in a quieter, lower tone than usual. Miss Allen knew what that meant without being told, and what the little girl wanted, and how the little heart was longing for something to rest upon, something to satisfy it,—longing for forgiveness, longing for peace, longing for Jesus. So, week after week she spoke about Him,—the One, the only One, the loving Saviour,—who calls the sinful and sorrowful ones to come to Him. And she told Annie that the wish to come was only the echo of His call, and that no one ever wanted to come but when He was calling them, just as she never heard the echo from the side of Elbury but when a strong, clear voice rang out to awake it. Then, if He wanted people to come to Him, it must be because He loved them. "You would not want me to come to the rectory, Annie, if you did not love me?" To this, and to all that might have called forth an answer, Annie only replied by pressing the hand which she held, and now and then with "You darling!" which to some persons might have passed for no answer at all, but Miss Allen knew better. But when the birthday came with which this chapter began, a different and fuller answer was given.

It was Annie's birthday request that Miss Allen might come to tea, if only she would. She came soon after dinner, so as to have a long afternoon, for Annie was not the only one who wanted "a talk with Miss Allen." In honour of the day, however, her great privilege was conceded, that she should have Miss Allen "all to herself for a bit" at first. So the kind friend allowed herself to be led to the drawing-room, where no one else was to come till Annie had had a reasonable share of her. The lamps were not lit, for the firelight was too pleasant to be interfered with sooner than was necessary! How glad Annie was to sit at her feet, and feel her hand stroking her hair, and resting gently and lovingly on her forehead. Even more so than usual, for it had been an unusually sad and weary day to Annie. She had wandered into the room where that day last year her dear suffering mamma's sweet birthday kiss had been given her, and then rushed away again, lest she should be found there. She could not settle to anything; she had no lessons to do, no book that she much cared to read, no amusement that seemed worth trying; the hours were long and heavy, and full of sad thoughts. That was no wonder, you will say. Yet the saddest were not because her dear mamma was gone to heaven. There was a darker thought still. What if she should never see her again? Even that was not quite the darkest. What if, after all dear Miss Allen had said to her, she should never be saved at all, never be able to love and praise the Saviour, never see Him in His beauty, but go on always fearful and unhappy, with a feeling of being "far off" all her life, and at last be lost for ever! She had prayed over and over again, but she did not feel sure she was heard, and felt almost sure she was not answered. She had asked the Lord Jesus to wash away all her sins in His precious blood; but how should she ever know that He had! Even when the thought came like a gleam of light, "Perhaps I *am* forgiven, and safe, though I don't know it!" it was quickly followed by another, "But perhaps I am not!" and then all was darkness and sadness again. So she longed for the afternoon, when Miss Allen would be almost sure to talk to her again about the things for which she cared more and more every day; and before she went down-stairs to meet her, she shut the door of her little room, and prayed, "O Lord, do save me; do forgive me! I do so want to love Thee; oh, do change my heart and make me good and happy! And oh! do grant that Miss Allen may talk to me, and let it do me good; for Jesus Christ's sake."

So Miss Allen and Annie sat together, and Miss Allen began to tell her about a little girl whom she had taught years before, and who had died very happily, mentioning some of the sweet and holy things she said. Annie listened sorrowfully; it all made her feel how different it was with her, and how little she could enter into the dying child's happy, quiet trust in the Good Shepherd. Tears began to trickle through her fingers as she hid her face in her hands, and bent her head lower and lower by Miss Allen's knee. At last she could bear it no longer, and with a great effort said, "Oh, Miss Allen, I wish—I wish I were good!"

"So do I, my pet," she answered; "I wish I were good, so we are wishing together."

"Oh, but, dear Miss Allen, I don't mean that; you know what I mean, only I did not like to put it in other words. It is—oh, Miss Allen!—if I did but know Jesus would love me and save me, and if I could but love Him!"

She had never spoken out in this way before. Miss Allen did not seem to keep her waiting, and yet there was time for a prayer that she might be guided to say the right thing to the poor little anxious heart.

"What would you give to know it, Annie?"

"Oh, *everything*! I *mean* it."

"Everything means a great deal, Annie; it means your home and everybody whom you love, even your dear papa. Do you mean *really* everything?—that you would rather love Jesus and know He loves you than keep all these?"

"Oh, Miss Allen, if you only knew! oh, indeed, indeed I would!"

She said slowly, and very firmly, "Then, Annie, dear child, I believe that it will not be very long before the Lord Jesus takes away the doubt and sorrow. I believe He will very soon make you see that He loves you, and then you will know that you love Him, and the fear will be gone."

Annie raised her head, and looked up at the earnest, loving face and undoubting eyes, which added to the force of the words.

"Annie, this longing for Jesus is because He is drawing you to Himself. And why is He drawing you?"

Annie did not answer. She knew Miss Allen would give the answer if she did not; but a thrill of hope came over her as she listened eagerly for it.

"Truly and only because He loves you, Annie,—*loves* you. And do you think He will let you be lost when He loves you?"

Annie's answer was first a smile, then an utterly sorrowful look, which said as plainly as words could have said, "But I can't quite believe it; and perhaps I shall be lost after all!"

Miss Allen read the look, and said, "It is that you do not trust the Lord Jesus,—you do not quite believe that He means what He says. Why won't you trust Him, Annie?"

The tears came again, and she said, "I can't bear not to trust Him. I don't know why I don't; but I don't, I know, else I should be happy."

"Annie, listen."

There was little need to tell her to listen, for the tone and manner almost made her hold her breath.

"Listen, and do not answer me, but think. If the Lord Jesus came now—now this moment—came in His glory, and you saw Him,—Jesus Himself,—

the same Jesus who said "Come unto Me,"—could you not trust yourself to *Him*—to HIM?"

There was silence. Annie's heart had an answer which just then she could not give even to Miss Allen,—an answer which could only be given to One, could only be laid at His feet who had put it into her friend's heart to ask that question, and sent the power of His Spirit with it.

She rose without a word, only stayed for one quick, fond kiss, and ran away to her own room, to kneel alone with Jesus. To that solemn appeal the answer had flashed up, strong and happy, "I could, oh, surely I could! How could I *not* trust Him if He came and I saw Him?—Him—Jesus Himself! Oh, if I could but see Him now!" And then came the impulse to go away at once, and kneel before Him, and tell Him she would doubt His love no longer—just to throw herself at His feet, with all her naughtiness and all her fears, and tell Him she loved Him.

Long she knelt by the little bed, telling Him this and much more, and wondering how it was that she never trusted herself to Him before. It was so new and so joyful to say, "Jesus, *dear* Saviour!" The very words were sweet as she looked up through the dusk, and reverently whispered them; and the thought that she had come to Him, and that He had graciously received her, was sweeter still. There could be no mistake about it, for it was Himself and no other who said, "Him that cometh to me I will in no wise cast out." She had come, and He could not have cast her out while His words stood certain and true. She had doubted them long enough; she would trust them now. And in so doing she found rest,—the rest she had heard of and could hardly imagine, because it seemed so far out of her reach. But the Lord Jesus is *always* true to His word, even to little children. There is rest, sweet rest and peace, for them as well as for older people. Ask Him to give it you, dear little ones; come to Him for it, and you will not be disappointed.

Annie came down to tea quiet and bright. Everything looked pleasant to her, for there was sunshine within which shone brighter than any lamp on that dark December evening. Strangers would have remarked nothing; neither did her sisters, who were busily planning sundry Christmas arrangements as to distribution of gifts in the parish, in conclave with the curate and Miss Allen, whose district was the largest and poorest. But Miss Allen marked the satisfied, happy look, and recognised it. She "took knowledge" of her that she "had been with Jesus."

Annie stayed up to supper that night, by special request of the curate, who said it was too bad to send anybody off to bed at eight o'clock, when it was the only birthday they had all the year round.

After supper, Miss Allen went to put on her bonnet, and Mary was going up-stairs with her; but Miss Allen playfully declined her attendance, and said Annie ought to pay for her supper by acting lady's maid after it, so Mary resigned in Annie's favour. It was a very little thing to do for dear Miss Allen, just to find her gloves, and hand her her bonnet, but it was more than ever a pleasure. When she was ready, she took both Annie's hands, and kissed her, and said, "Annie, I have not forgotten about your four happy days; have you?" "No, Miss Allen." "Dearie, I have been so sorry for you, for I knew they could not be what you expected, and *one* ——" She did not say more about that one, the saddest of all, but broke off, and said, "This was the fourth, was it not? And I think this has been a happy one. Tell me, darling, has it not?"

Annie threw her arms round Miss Allen's neck, and said, "Oh, I can't think why I never trusted Him before! I can love Him now, and I do. This is the happiest of all the happy days I ever had, and I thought it was going to be such an unhappy one. Oh, Miss Allen, how good the Lord Jesus is!"

Jesus, I will trust Thee, trust Thee with my soul;
Guilty, lost, and helpless, Thou canst make me whole.
There is none in heaven or on earth like Thee,
Thou hast died for sinners, therefore, Lord, for me.

Jesus, I may trust Thee, name of matchless worth!
Spoken by the angel at Thy wondrous birth;
Written, and for ever, on Thy cross of shame,
Sinners read, and worship, trusting in that name.

Jesus, I must trust Thee, pondering Thy ways:
Full of love and mercy, all Thine earthly days,
Sinners gathered round Thee, lepers sought Thy face,—
None too vile or loathsome for a Saviour's grace.

Jesus, I can trust Thee, trust Thy written word,
Though Thy voice of pity I have never heard.
When Thy Spirit teacheth, to my taste how sweet!
Only may I hearken, sitting at Thy feet!

Jesus, I do trust Thee, trust without a doubt,
Whosoever cometh, Thou wilt not cast out!
Faithful is Thy promise, precious is Thy blood—
These my soul's salvation, Thou my Saviour-God!

Jesus, I Will Trust Thee

Words by Mary Jane (Deck) Walker
Music by Frances Ridley Havergal

1. Je - sus, I will trust Thee, trust Thee with my soul;

Guil - ty, lost, and help - less, Thou canst make me whole.

There is none in hea - ven or on earth like Thee.

Thou hast died for sin - ners, there-fore, Lord, for me. A - men.

Wayside Chimes. May.

Love for love.

"We have known & believed the love that God hath to us." I John 4.16

Knowing that the God on high,
With a tender Father's grace,
Waits to hear your faintest cry,
Waits to show a Father's face, —
Stay & think! oh should not you
Love this gracious Father too?

Knowing Christ was crucified,
Knowing that He loves you now
Just as much as when He died
With the thorns upon His brow, —
Stay & think! oh should not you
Love this blessed Saviour too?

Knowing that the Spirit strives
With your weary, wandering heart,
Who would change the restless lives,
Pure & perfect peace impart, —
Stay & think! oh should not you
Love this loving Spirit too?

Frances Ridley Havergal

A fair copy autograph of "Love for Love" by F.R.H., written February 12, 1879. See page iii.

Made in the USA
San Bernardino, CA
06 June 2020